THE PSALMS:
A NEW TRANSLATION

This translation of the Psalms is inspired by the work of R. Tournay o.p., Raymond Schwab, J. Gelineau s.j., T. G. Chifflot o.p., who were responsible for the translation of the *Bible de Jérusalem* Psalms from Hebrew into French and had the happy thought of bringing the rhythmic pattern of the Hebrew into their rendering. This version attempts to do the same in English.

The Grail would like to record their debt to these four French scholars and to acknowledge their appreciation of the consistent encouragement which they have received during every stage of the work.

This translation, which is also made from the Hebrew, is the work of a team of scholars in co-operation with *The Grail*, which has already brought out a musical edition of some fifty of these psalms.

THE PSALMS
A NEW TRANSLATION

TRANSLATED FROM THE HEBREW
AND ARRANGED FOR SINGING
TO THE PSALMODY OF
JOSEPH GELINEAU

Collins

FONTANA BOOKS

First published in Fontana Books, September 1963
Ninth Impression February 1974

Imprimatur
✠ GULIELMUS CARD. GODFREY
Archiepŭs Westmonast.
Datum Westmon. die 25a Martii 1962

© THE GRAIL (*England*) *1963*
Printed in Great Britain
Collins Clear-Type Press
London and Glasgow

INTRODUCTION

1. The Songs of Israel

The 150 poems which make up the book of psalms sing to us the human and divine history of Israel.

A psalm is a religious song. The very word "psalm" suggests a musical instrument, tambourine or sistrum, harp or primitive lyre, with which the singer accompanied his song. The psalmist recited the verses to a simple chant, some echoes of which can doubtless be heard in certain Jewish and Christian psalmodies. These verses showed a balanced symmetry of form and sense, they scanned rhythmically in three, four or five feet, and were linked in more or less frequent stanzas. When he speaks a whole world of images rises from his words as they call to each other, repeating, following or clashing with each other. He makes his point not by reasoning but by hammering; he reveals not by describing but by actually touching; he teaches not by explaining but by putting his words on our lips.

The psalms are a series of shouts : shouts of love and hatred; shouts of suffering or rejoicing; shouts of faith or hope. Here, a man who has suffered injury demands justice (Ps. 55) or the whole defeated nation laments (Ps. 43); there, a sick man who has escaped death gives thanks (Ps. 29) or the whole people proclaim that the hand of God alone has rescued them from foreign slavery (Ps. 80). Wise men meditate on the Law, the charter of the covenant between God and his people (Ps. 118), and choirs celebrate the power and holiness of the Lord who overthrows the strong and raises up the humble (Ps. 146).

How were these poems born? Where, when and by whom were they written? Tradition attributes them to King David "the singer of the songs of Israel" (2 Sam. 23 : 1) or to the musicians' guilds connected with the names of Asaph or Korah. There is no doubt that the psalm *genre* goes back very far in the history of Israel and that David excelled in the art. Nevertheless it is no longer possible to attach a date or author to each psalm. This is less important than the fact that Israel has preserved these poems because it has recognised in them the expression of its unique religious destiny. The psalms repeat in lyrical form the teaching of the prophets; they recall the great events of a history that was itself a divine revelation; they meditate on the covenant.

The collection of the psalms into five books was possibly made for liturgical purposes. It was compiled after the return from the Babylonian captivity and was completed by the third century before Christ. A great number of the psalms belong to this post-exile period, but some are clearly earlier, and recall the period of the Kings (e.g. Ps. 19-20). In the controversial matter of psalm chronology, we should forget neither the enduring character of an age-old literary form, which lends itself to creative imitation, nor the progressive nature of a revelation which continued to inform the ancient formulas with an ever clearer messianic consciousness.

2. Prophecy and Christ's Prayer

On Easter night, when the redemption had been accomplished in the death and resurrection of Christ, Jesus said to his apostles : " This is what I told you while I still walked in your company; how all that was written of me in the law of Moses, and in the prophets, and in the psalms, must be fulfilled." (Luke 24 :44). In Christ the full significance of the songs of Israel is revealed; they announced the Word of Life. He personally described himself as the Lord whom God seated at his right hand (Ps. 109, Matt. 22 :44); as the stone rejected by the builders which became the head of the corner (Ps. 117, Matt. 21 :42); as he who comes, blessed in the name of the Lord (Ps. 117, Matt. 23 :39. He personally applied to himself on the cross the appeal of the persecuted psalmist (Ps. 21, Matt. 27 :46) and his prayer of trust (Ps. 30, Luke 23 :46).

Everything that the psalms had sung about Yahweh the God of Israel, as the one who judges and saves his people, who comes to dwell among them, who reveals his Law to them, gathers them together, leads and sanctifies them, all that finds its expression and its accomplishment in the Incarnate Word. Since then we know the " Lord " of the psalms and " have seen his glory " : it is Jesus the Son

6

of David and the Son of God, who judges the world in his death, who saves it in his resurrection, who has become man among us and has made the Father known to us; he is the Truth, the Way and the Life of which the psalms speak.

God and Saviour, Jesus is also the Son of Man, recapitulating in the passover of his death and resurrection the whole destiny of mankind. The appeal of the just man under persecution and the cry of the suffering servant are more fitting on his lips than on those of any of the afflicted people of Israel; and his resurrection gives more meaning to redeemed humanity's song of thanksgiving than any short-lived delivery from evil in the Old Testament. The psalms, expressing as they do man's attitude before God, find the fullness of their meaning in the new Adam. Henceforth we recognise in Christ the God of the psalms. Henceforth the voice of the psalmist is the voice of Christ.

3. The Psalms in the Preaching and the Prayer of the Church

Enlightened by the Spirit of Pentecost the apostles saw the mysteries of Christ foreshadowed in these inspired poems. In their preaching Peter and Paul used these familiar texts to show that what they pointed to had been fulfilled in the risen Christ (Acts 2:25-35; Acts 13:33; Eph. 4:8 etc.). All their successors—Justin, Hippolytus, Hilary, Augustine—give the psalms the same privileged place in their preaching of the Gospel. All the Christian liturgies make the psalter their first source for texts to celebrate the mysteries of the Lord, his birth (Ps. 2:7); his manifestation to the Gentiles (Ps. 97:2); his sufferings and death (Ps. 21); his resurrection (Ps. 117); his ascension (Ps. 46), and his second coming to judge all men (Ps. 95).

It is not surprising therefore that Christ's Church should have found in the psalms her favourite prayer. These inspired verses resound in the liturgy of the Word, in the celebration of the Mass, in the Divine Office, and in the most varied ceremonies of every rite. The Bride delights to use the words of the Spirit. At one moment she uses them to praise her heavenly Lord, at another she identifies her voice with that of the mediator, the true and universal

7

psalmist, in order to pray to the Father. Yet again she turns towards Christ, God made man, to ask for help or to give him thanks.

For the Church is the new Israel and the new people of God. As the Body of the risen Christ, she is the true Temple; as the assembly of believers, she is the new Jerusalem. Through the images of the old covenant the Church gives voice to the invisible realities of the new covenant.

4. The Psalms in our Prayer

"We were born with this book in our very bones. A small book; 150 poems; 150 steps between death and life; 150 mirrors of our rebellions and our loyalties, of our agonies and our resurrections. More than a book, it is a living being who speaks, who suffers, groans and dies, who rises again and speaks on the threshold of eternity; who seizes one, bears one away, oneself and all the ages of time, from the beginning to the end." (A. Chouraqi).

No one who takes the words of the psalms on his lips and their meaning in his heart, who allows the rhythm of their images to take hold of him and their accents to echo through his being, can possibly remain indifferent to them. They may overwhelm or shock, bring peace or exaltation, but inevitably they draw us beyond ourselves; they force us to that meeting with the God without whom we cannot live and who transforms our whole life. The psalms compel us to belief and hope.

Some may object that certain passages contradict the command of love taught us by Christ. But we have only to follow the images through to their Easter fulfilment in Christ's passover, and to ask ourselves what it is that the psalmist loves and hates, to realise that the choice no longer lies between friends or enemies, but between the reign of evil which holds sway in us and the reign of grace which lays claim to us. If these words leave us unmoved it means that we are incapable of hatred and consequently of love. If they are a stumbling block for us, it means that the man of the Old Testament is still sleeping within us though we claim to be disciples of Christ.

Others raise different objections: they don't care to join the psalmist in proclaiming their own innocence or loyalty;

8

they don't want to pray in terms of an anguish they have not experienced, or give thanks with a jubilation they have never felt. But do such people think that the prayers they use are merely their own prayers? Do they not realise that they stand before God in the company of the whole of mankind? Their prayer is that of the whole Church and it only reaches the Father through the voice of Christ the Mediator. The psalms compel us to voice all the prayer of the people of God and of their Head; they force us to widen our hearts to the full dimensions of the redemption. They make us say what remains hidden except to the eyes of faith, and what we know we must one day become.

5. Ancient and Modern Versions

God speaks to man in human words. The revelation contained in holy Scripture can only reach the men to whom it is addressed if it uses the languages they speak.

More than two centuries before Christ the book of psalms was translated into Greek in Alexandria. This Septuagint version was used by the authors of the New Testament for their preaching of Christianity, and it continued to serve as a basis for most of the ancient translations of the psalms, in particular for the most widespread of the Latin versions, known as the Vulgate. It is readily understandable that the Septuagint continues to retain a special authority in the Church.[1]

However, as a result of progress in biblical studies, almost all modern versions of the psalms are to-day based on the original text. This recourse to the Hebrew allows the translator to stay close to this unique literary form, with its repetition of words, its own particular images, its stylistic peculiarities and its poetic rhythm. The translation of a poem cannot be made simply by a faithful rendering of its meaning. The whole character of the original language must be conveyed. When it is a matter of the word of God, where the historical nature of revelation has made content and form even more inseparable, the need for literary fidelity takes on special importance; though this does not mean that the ancient versions may be neglected, witnessing as they do to the way in which the Church has interpreted the inspired text.

It is this literary fidelity which was aimed at in the

French Version of the *Bible de Jérusalem* (1st edition by R. Tournay and R. Schwab, Paris 1950; 2nd edition with the collaboration of J. Gelineau and T. G. Chifflot, Paris 1955). Special attention was paid to the rhythmic structure of the poetry of the psalms, and this allowed a sung or recited psalmody to be fashioned on the basis of the analogy that exists between the Hebrew tonic rhythm and that of our modern languages.

Since 1953 this new way of singing the psalms has spread rapidly among French Catholics. Following the success of the French venture, The Grail took the initiative in making an English translation based on the same principles. The work was begun in 1954 with the collaboration of Gall Schuon, o.c.s.o., Albert Derzelle, o.c.s.o., and Hubert Richards, L.S.S., for the translation from the original texts, of Philippa Craig for the literary style, and (in the musical editionss) of Gregory Murray, o.s.b. for the " singability." The first collection of 24 psalms appeared in 1956 and a further collection of 30 psalms in 1958, both collections being arranged for singing. The whole 150 have now been translated and appear in this volume. From the efforts of this team has come a translation which Professor H. H. Rowley has described as " a very impressive rendering " for which he has " nothing but praise ".

At a time when those who profess Jesus Christ as their only Saviour are searching for the things that will end their separation and unite them, may the inspired poetry of the psalms allow all of them to sing in the same words and in the same Spirit their common faith in the same Lord.

J. GELINEAU

A note on the numbering of the psalms and verses will be found on page 255.

I

Two ways of living

1 Happy indeed is the man
who follows not the counsel of the wicked;
nor lingers in the way of sinners
nor sits in the company of scorners,
2 but whose delight is the law of the Lord
and who ponders his law day and night.

3 He is like a tree that is planted
beside the flowing waters,
that yields its fruit in due season
and whose leaves shall never fade;
and all that he does shall prosper.
4 Not so are the wicked, not so!

For they like winnowed chaff
shall be driven away by the wind.
5 When the wicked are judged they shall not stand,
nor find room among those who are just;
6 for the Lord guards the way of the just
but the way of the wicked leads to doom.

2

The Messianic kingship:
warning to rulers and nations

1 Why this tumult among nations,
  among peoples this useless murmuring?
2 They arise, the kings of the earth,
  princes plot against the Lord and his Anointed.
3 "Come, let us break their fetters,
  come, let us cast off their yoke."

4 He who sits in the heavens laughs;
  the Lord is laughing them to scorn.
5 Then he will speak in his anger,
  his rage will strike them with terror.
6 "It is I who who have set up my king
  on Sion, my holy mountain."

7 (I will announce the decree of the Lord:)

  The Lord said to me: "You are my Son.
  It is I who have begotten you this day.
8 Ask and I shall bequeath you the nations,
  put the ends of the earth in your possession.
9 With a rod of iron you will break them,
  shatter them like a potter's jar."

10 Now, O kings, understand,
   take warning, rulers of the earth;
11 serve the Lord with awe
   and trembling, pay him your homage
12 lest he be angry and you perish;
   for suddenly his anger will blaze.

  Blessed are they who put their trust in God.

3

Confidence under persecution:
a morning prayer

2 How many are my foes, O Lord!
  How many are rising up against me!
3 How many are saying about me:
  "There is no help for him in God."

4 But you, Lord, are a shield about me,
  my glory, who lift up my head.
5 I cry aloud to the Lord.
  He answers from his holy mountain.

6 I lie down to rest and I sleep.
  I wake, for the Lord upholds me.
7 I will not fear even thousands of people
  who are ranged on every side against me.

8 Arise, Lord; save me, my God,
  you who strike all my foes on the mouth,
  you who break the teeth of the wicked!
9 O Lord of salvation, bless your people!

4

Night prayer

2 When I call, answer me, O God of justice;
  from anguish you released me, have mercy and hear
    me!

3 O men, how long will your hearts be closed,
  will you love what is futile and seek what is false

4 It is the Lord who grants favours to those whom he
    loves;
  the Lord hears me whenever I call him.

5 Fear him; do not sin : ponder on your bed and be still.
6 Make justice your sacrifice and trust in the Lord.

7 "What can bring us happiness?" many say.
  Lift up the light of your face on us, O Lord.

8 You have put into my heart a greater joy
  than they have from abundance of corn and new wine.

9 I will lie down in peace and sleep comes at once
  for you alone, Lord, make me dwell in safety.

5

Morning prayer

2 To my words give ear, O Lord,
  give heed to my groaning.
3 Attend to the sound of my cries,
  my King and my God.

  It is you whom I invoke, 4 O Lord.
  In the morning you hear me;
  in the morning I offer you my prayer,
  watching and waiting.

5 You are no God who loves evil;
  no sinner is your guest.
6 The boastful shall not stand their ground
  before your face.

7 You hate all who do evil:
  you destroy all who lie.
  The deceitful and bloodthirsty man
  the Lord detests.

8 But I through the greatness of your love
  have access to your house.
  I bow down before your holy temple,
  filled with awe.

9 Lead me, Lord, in your justice,
  because of those who lie in wait;
  make clear your way before me.

10 No truth can be found in their mouths,
   their heart is all mischief,
   their throat a wide-open grave,
   all honey their speech.

11 Declare them guilty, O God.
   Let them fail in their designs.
   Drive them out for their many offences:
   for they have defied you.

12 All those you protect shall be glad
   and ring out their joy.
   You shelter them; in you they rejoice,
   those who love your name.

13 It is you who bless the just man, Lord:
   you surround him with favour as with a shield.

6

Prayer in time of distress:
first psalm of repentance

2 Lord, do not reprove me in your anger;
  punish me not in your rage.
3 Have mercy on me, Lord, I have no strength;
  Lord, heal me, my body is racked;
4 my soul is racked with pain.

  But you, O Lord . . . how long?
5 Return, Lord, rescue my soul.
  Save me in your merciful love;
6 for in death no one remembers you;
  from the grave, who can give you praise?

7 I am exhausted with my groaning;
  every night I drench my pillow with tears;
  I bedew my bed with weeping.
8 My eye wastes away with grief;
  I have grown old surrounded by my foes.

9 Leave me, all you who do evil;
  for the Lord has heard my weeping.
10 The Lord has heard my plea;
  The Lord will accept my prayer.
11 All my foes will retire in confusion,
  foiled and suddenly confounded.

7

Appeal to God's justice

2 Lord God, I take refuge in you.
From my pursuer save me and rescue me,
3 lest he tear me to pieces like a lion
and drag me off with no one to rescue me

4 Lord God, if my hands have done wrong,
5 if I have paid back evil for good,
I who saved my unjust oppressor:
6 then let my foe pursue me and seize me,
let him trample my life to the ground
and lay my soul in the dust.

* * *

7 Lord, rise up in your anger,
rise against the fury of my foes;
my God, awake! You will give judgment.
8 Let the company of nations gather round you,
taking your seat above them on high.
9 (The Lord is judge of the peoples.)

Give judgment for me, Lord; I am just
and innocent of heart.
10 Put an end to the evil of the wicked!
Make the just stand firm,
you who test mind and heart,
O just God!

11 God is the shield that protects me,
who saves the upright of heart.
12 God is a just judge
slow to anger;
but he threatens the wicked every day,
13 men who will not repent.

* * *

God will sharpen his sword;
he has braced his bow and taken aim.
14 For them he has prepared deadly weapons;
he barbs his arrows with fire.
15 Here is one who is pregnant with malice,
conceives evil and brings forth lies.

16 He digs a pitfall, digs it deep;
and in the trap he has made he will fall.
17 His malice will recoil on himself;
on his own head his violence will fall.

* * *

18 I will thank the Lord for his justice:
I will sing to the Lord, the Most High.

8

Man the viceroy of God

2 How great is your name, O Lord our God,
 through all the earth!

 Your majesty is praised above the heavens;
3 on the lips of children and of babes
 you have found praise to foil your enemy,
 to silence the foe and the rebel.

4 When I see the heavens, the work of your hands,
 the moon and the stars which you arranged,
5 what is man that you should keep him in mind,
 mortal man that you care for him?

6 Yet you have made him little less than a god;
 with glory and honour you crowned him,
7 gave him power over the works of your hand,
 put all things under his feet.

8 All of them, sheep and cattle,
 yes, even the savage beasts,
9 birds of the air, and fish
 that make their way through the waters.

10 How great is your name, O Lord our God,
 through all the earth!

9

Gratitude and appeal:
an alphabetical psalm

2 I will praise you, Lord, with all my heart;
  I will recount all your wonders.
3 I will rejoice in you and be glad,
  and sing psalms to your name, O Most High.

4 See how my enemies turn back,
  how they stumble and perish before you.
5 You upheld the justice of my cause;
  you sat enthroned, judging with justice.

6 You have checked the nations, destroyed the wicked;
  you have wiped out their name for ever and ever.
7 The foe is destroyed, eternally ruined.
  You uprooted their cities; their memory has perished.

8 But the Lord sits enthroned for ever.
  He has set up his throne for judgment;
9 he will judge the world with justice,
  he will judge the peoples with his truth.

10 For the oppressed let the Lord be a stronghold,
  a stronghold in times of distress.
11 Those who know your name will trust you:
  you will never forsake those who seek you.

12 Sing psalms to the Lord who dwells in Sion.
  Proclaim his mighty works among the peoples;
13 for the Avenger of blood has remembered them,
  and has not forgotten the cry of the poor.

14 Have pity on me, Lord, see my sufferings,
  you who save me from the gates of death;
15 that I may recount all your praise
  at the gates of the city of Sion
  and rejoice in your saving help.

16 The nations have fallen in the pit which they made,
their feet caught in the snare they laid.
17 The Lord has revealed himself, and given judgment.
The wicked are snared in the work of their own hands.

18 Let the wicked go down among the dead,
all the nations forgetful of God.
19 For the needy shall not always be forgotten
nor the hopes of the poor be in vain.

20 Arise, Lord, let men not prevail!
Let the nations be judged before you.
21 Lord, strike them with terror,
let the nations know they are but men.

(*Here, in the Hebrew text, Psalm* 10 *begins*)

1 Lord, why do you stand afar off
and hide yourself in times of distress?
2 The poor man is devoured by the pride of the wicked:
he is caught in the schemes that others have made.

3 For the wicked man boasts of his heart's desires;
the covetous blasphemes and spurns the Lord.
4 In his pride the wicked says: "He will not punish.
There is no God." Such are his thoughts.

5 His path is ever untroubled;
your judgment is far from his mind.
His enemies he regards with contempt.
6 He thinks: "Never shall I falter:
misfortune shall never be my lot."

7 His mouth is full of cursing, guile, oppression,
mischief and deceit under his tongue.
8 He lies in wait among the reeds;
the innocent he murders in secret.

His eyes are on the watch for the helpless man.
9 He lurks in hiding like a lion in his lair;
he lurks in hiding to seize the poor;
he seizes the poor man and drags him away.

10 He crouches, preparing to spring,
   and the helpless fall beneath his strength.
11 He thinks in his heart: "God forgets,
   he hides his face, he does not see."

12 Arise then, Lord, lift up your hand!
   O God, do not forget the poor!
13 Why should the wicked spurn the Lord
   and think in his heart: "He will not punish"?

14 But you have seen the trouble and sorrow,
   you note it, you take it in hand.
   The helpless trusts himself to you;
   for you are the helper of the orphan.

15 Break the power of the wicked and the sinner!
   Punish his wickedness till nothing remains!
16 The Lord is king for ever and ever.
   The heathen shall perish from the land he rules.

17 Lord, you hear the prayer of the poor;
   you strengthen their hearts; you turn your ear
18 to protect the rights of the orphan and oppressed:
   so that mortal man may strike terror no more.

10

The security of God's friends:
a psalm of confidence

1 In the Lord I have taken my refuge.
  How can you say to my soul:
  "Fly like a bird to its mountain.

2 See the wicked bracing their bow;
  they are fixing their arrows on the string
  to shoot upright men in the dark.
3 Foundations once destroyed, what can the just do?""

4 The Lord is in his holy temple,
  the Lord, whose throne is in heaven.
  His eyes look down on the world;
  his gaze tests mortal men.

5 The Lord tests the just and the wicked:
  the lover of violence he hates.
6 He sends fire and brimstone on the wicked;
  he sends a scorching wind as their lot.

7 The Lord is just and loves justice:
  the upright shall see his face.

Truth in a world of lies

2 Help, O Lord, for good men have vanished:
  truth has gone from the sons of men.
3 Falsehood they speak one to another,
  with lying lips, with a false heart.

4 May the Lord destroy all lying lips,
  the tongue speaking high-sounding words,
5 those who say: "Our tongue is our strength;
  our lips are our own, who is our master?"

6 "For the poor who are oppressed and the needy who
    groan
  I myself will arise," says the Lord.
  "I will grant them the salvation for which they thirst."

7 The words of the Lord are words without alloy,
  silver from the furnace, seven times refined.

8 It is you, O Lord, who will take us in your care
  and protect us for ever from this generation.
9 See how the wicked prowl on every side,
  while the worthless are prized highly by the sons of
    men.

12

Prayer of a man in anxiety

2 How long, O Lord, will you forget me?
  How long will you hide your face?
3 How long must I bear grief in my soul,
  this sorrow in my heart day and night?
  How long shall my enemy prevail?

4 Look at me, answer me, Lord my God!
  Give light to my eyes lest I fall asleep in death,
5 lest my enemy say: "I have overcome him";
  lest my foes rejoice to see my fall.

6 As for me, I trust in your merciful love.
  Let my heart rejoice in your saving help:
7 Let me sing to the Lord for his goodness to me,
  singing psalms to the name of the Lord, the Most High.

13

The fools

1 The fool has said in his heart:
"There is no God above."
Their deeds are corrupt, depraved;
not a good man is left.

2 From heaven the Lord looks down
on the sons of men
to see if any are wise,
if any seek God.

3 All have left the right path,
depraved, every one:
there is not a good man left,
no, not even one.

4 Will the evil-doers not understand?
They eat up my people
as though they ate bread:
they never pray to the Lord.

5 See how they tremble with fear
without cause for fear:
for God is with the just.
6 You may mock the poor man's hope,
but his refuge is the Lord.

7 O that Israel's salvation might come from Sion!
When the Lord delivers his people from bondage,
then Jacob will be glad and Israel rejoice.

14

Moral code of a good man

1 Lord, who shall be admitted to your tent
and dwell on your holy mountain?

2 He who walks without fault;
he who acts with justice
and speaks the truth from his heart;
3 he who does not slander with his tongue;

he who does no wrong to his brother,
who casts no slur on his neighbour,
4 who holds the godless in disdain,
but honours those who fear the Lord;

he who keeps his pledge, come what may;
5 who takes no interest on a loan
and accepts no bribes against the innocent.
Such a man will stand firm for ever.

15

True happiness:
a psalm of confidence

1 Preserve me, God, I take refuge in you.
2 I say to the Lord: "You are my God.
  My happiness lies in you alone."

3 He has put into my heart a marvellous love
  for the faithful ones who dwell in his land.
4 Those who choose other gods increase their sorrows.
  Never will I offer their offerings of blood.
  Never will I take their name upon my lips.

5 O Lord, it is you who are my portion and cup;
  it is you yourself who are my prize.
6 The lot marked out for me is my delight:
  welcome indeed the heritage that falls to me!

7 I will bless the Lord who gives me counsel,
  who even at night directs my heart.
8 I keep the Lord ever in my sight:
  since he is at my right hand, I shall stand firm.

9 And so my heart rejoices, my soul is glad;
  even my body shall rest in safety.
10 For you will not leave my soul among the dead,
  nor let your beloved know decay.

11 You will show me the path of life,
  the fullness of joy in your presence,
  at your right hand happiness for ever.

16

Appeal of an upright man

1 Lord, hear a cause that is just,
   pay heed to my cry.
   Turn your ear to my prayer:
   no deceit is on my lips.
2 From you may my judgment come forth.
   Your eyes discern the truth.

3 You search my heart, you visit me by night.
   You test me and you find in me no wrong.
   My words are not sinful 4 as are men's words.

   I kept from violence because of your word,
5 I kept my feet firmly in your paths;
   there was no faltering in my steps.

6 I am here and I call, you will hear me, O God.
   Turn your ear to me; hear my words.
7 Display your great love, you whose right hand saves
   your friends from those who rebel against them.

8 Guard me as the apple of your eye.
   Hide me in the shadow of your wings
9 from the violent attack of the wicked.

   My foes encircle me with deadly intent.
10 Their hearts tight shut, their mouths speak proudly.
11 They advance against me, and now they surround me.

   Their eyes are watching to strike me to the ground
12 as though they were lions ready to claw
   or like some young lion crouched in hiding.

13 Lord, arise, confront them, strike them down!
   Let your sword rescue my soul from the wicked;
14 let your hand, O Lord, rescue me from men,
   from men whose reward is in this present life.

You give them their fill of your treasures;
they rejoice in abundance of offspring
and leave their wealth to their children.

15 As for me, in my justice I shall see your face
and be filled, when I awake, with the sight of your
glory.

17

David's gratitude for victory

2 I love you, Lord, my strength,
3 my rock, my fortress, my saviour.
  My God is the rock where I take refuge;
  my shield, my mighty help, my stronghold.
4 The Lord is worthy of all praise :
  when I call I am saved from my foes.

5 The waves of death rose about me;
  the torrents of destruction assailed me;
6 the snares of the grave entangled me;
  the traps of death confronted me.

7 In my anguish I called to the Lord;
  I cried to my God for help.
  From his temple he heard my voice;
  my cry came to his ears.

8 Then the earth reeled and rocked;
  the mountains were shaken to their base :
  they reeled at his terrible anger.
9 Smoke came forth from his nostrils
  and scorching fire from his mouth :
  coals were set ablaze by its heat.

10 He lowered the heavens and came down,
   a black cloud under his feet.
11 He came enthroned on the cherubim,
   he flew on the wings of the wind.

12 He made the darkness his covering,
   the dark waters of the clouds, his tent.
13 A brightness shone out before him
   with hailstones and flashes of fire.

14 The Lord thundered in the heavens;
   the Most High let his voice be heard.
15 He shot his arrows, scattered the foe,
   flashed his lightnings, and put them to flight.

16 The bed of the ocean was revealed;
   the foundations of the world were laid bare
   at the thunder of your threat, O Lord,
   at the blast of the breath of your anger.

17 From on high he reached down and seized me;
   he drew me forth from the mighty waters.
18 He snatched me from my powerful foe,
   from my enemies whose strength I could not match.

19 They assailed me in the day of my misfortune,
   but the Lord was my support.
20 He brought me forth into freedom,
   he saved me because he loved me.

21 He rewarded me because I was just,
   repaid me, for my hands were clean,
22 for I have kept the way of the Lord
   and have not fallen away from my God.

23 For his judgments are all before me:
   I have never neglected his commands.
24 I have always been upright before him;
   I have kept myself from guilt.

25 He repaid me because I was just
   and my hands were clean in his eyes.
26 You are loving with those who love you:
   you show yourself perfect with the perfect.

27 With the sincere you show yourself sincere,
   but the cunning you outdo in cunning.
28 For you save a humble people
   but humble the eyes that are proud.

29 You, O Lord, are my lamp,
   my God who lightens my darkness.
30 With you I can break through any barrier,
   with my God I can scale any wall.

31 As for God, his ways are perfect;
   the word of the Lord, purest gold.
   He indeed is the shield
   of all who make him their refuge.

32 For who is God but the Lord?
Who is a rock but our God?
33 The God who girds me with strength
and makes the path safe before me.

34 My feet you made swift as the deer's;
you have made me stand firm on the heights.
35 You have trained my hands for battle
and my arms to bend the heavy bow.

36 You gave me your saving shield;
you upheld me, trained me with care.
37 You gave me freedom for my steps;
my feet have never slipped.

38 I pursued and overtook my foes,
never turning back till they were slain.
39 I smote them so they could not rise;
they fell beneath my feet.

40 You girded me with strength for battle;
you made my enemies fall beneath me,
41 you made my foes take flight;
those who hated me I destroyed.

42 They cried, but there was no one to save them;
they cried to the Lord, but in vain.
43 I crushed them fine as dust before the wind;
trod them down like dirt in the streets.

44 You saved me from the feuds of the people
and put me at the head of the nations.
People unknown to me served me:
45 when they heard of me they obeyed me.

Foreign nations came to me cringing:
46 foreign nations faded away.
They came trembling out of their strongholds.

47 Long life to the Lord, my rock!
Praised be the God who saves me,
48 the God who gives me redress
and subdues people under me.

49 You saved me from my furious foes.
   You set me above my assailants.
   You saved me from violent men,
50 so I will praise you, Lord, among the nations:
   I will sing a psalm to your name.

51 He has given great victories to his king
   and shown his love for his anointed,
   for David and his sons for ever.

18

Praise of God, creator and law-giver

2 The heavens proclaim the glory of God
  and the firmament shows forth the work of his hands.
3 Day unto day takes up the story
  and night unto night makes known the message.

4 No speech, no word, no voice is heard
5 yet their span goes forth through all the earth,
  their words to the utmost bounds of the world.

  There he has placed a tent for the sun;
6 it comes forth like a bridegroom coming from his tent,
  rejoices like a champion to run its course.

7 At the end of the sky is the rising of the sun;
  to the furthest end of the sky is its course.
  There is nothing concealed from its burning heat.

*   *   *

8 The law of the Lord is perfect,
  it revives the soul.
  The rule of the Lord is to be trusted,
  it gives wisdom to the simple.

9 The precepts of the Lord are right,
  they gladden the heart.
  The command of the Lord is clear,
  it gives light to the eyes.

10 The fear of the Lord is holy,
  abiding for ever.
  The decrees of the Lord are truth
  and all of them just.

11 They are more to be desired than gold,
   than the purest of gold
   and sweeter are they than honey,
   than honey from the comb.

12 So in them your servant finds instruction;
   great reward is in their keeping.
13 But who can detect all his errors?
   From hidden faults acquit me.

14 From presumption restrain your servant
   and let it not rule me.
   Then shall I be blameless,
   clean from grave sin.

15 May the spoken words of my mouth,
   the thoughts of my heart,
   win favour in your sight, O Lord,
   my rescuer, my rock!

19

Prayer for a king before battle

2 May the Lord answer in time of trial;
may the name of Jacob's God protect you.

3 May he send you help from his shrine
and give you support from Sion.
4 May he remember all your offerings
and receive your sacrifice with favour.

5 May he give you your heart's desire
and fulfil every one of your plans.
6 May we ring out our joy at your victory
and rejoice in the name of our God.
May the Lord grant all your prayers.

7 I am sure now that the Lord
will give victory to his anointed,
will reply from his holy heaven
with the mighty victory of his hand.

8 Some trust in chariots or horses,
but we in the name of the Lord.
9 They will collapse and fall,
but we shall hold and stand firm.

10 Give victory to the king, O Lord,
give answer on the day we call.

After victory

2 O Lord, your strength gives joy to the king;
   how your saving help makes him glad!
3 You have granted him his heart's desire;
   you have not refused the prayer of his lips.

4 You came to meet him with the blessings of success,
   you have set on his head a crown of pure gold.
5 He asked you for life and this you have given,
   days that will last from age to age.

6 Your saving help has given him glory.
   You have laid upon him majesty and splendour,
7 you have granted your blessings to him for ever.
   You have made him rejoice with the joy of your
      presence.

8 The king has put his trust in the Lord:
   through the mercy of the Most High he shall stand
      firm.
9 His hand will seek and find all his foes,
   his right hand find out those that hate him.

10 You will burn them like a blazing furnace
   on the day when you appear.
   And the Lord shall destroy them in his anger;
   fire will swallow them up.

11 You will wipe out their race from the earth
   and their children from the sons of men.
12 Though they plan evil against you,
   though they plot, they shall not prevail.

13 For you will force them to retreat;
   at them you will aim with your bow.
14 O Lord, arise in your strength;
   we shall sing and praise your power.

The suffering servant wins
the deliverance of the nations

2 My God, my God, why have you forsaken me?
  You are far from my plea and the cry of my distress.
3 O my God, I call by day and you give no reply;
  I call by night and I find no peace.

4 Yet you, O God, are holy,
  enthroned on the praises of Israel.
5 In you our fathers put their trust;
  they trusted and you set them free.
6 When they cried to you, they escaped.
  In you they trusted and never in vain.

7 But I am a worm and no man,
  the butt of men, laughing-stock of the people.
8 All who see me deride me.
  They curl their lips, they toss their heads.
9 "He trusted in the Lord, let him save him;
  let him release him if this is his friend."

10 Yes, it was you who took me from the womb,
  entrusted me to my mother's breast.
11 To you I was committed from my birth,
  from my mother's womb you have been my God.
12 Do not leave me alone in my distress;
  come close, there is none else to help.

13 Many bulls have surrounded me,
  fierce bulls of Bashan close me in.
14 Against me they open wide their jaws,
  like lions, rending and roaring.

15 Like water I am poured out,
  disjointed are all my bones.
  My heart has become like wax,
  it is melted within my breast.

16 Parched as burnt clay is my throat,
my tongue cleaves to my jaws.

17 Many dogs have surrounded me,
a band of the wicked beset me.
They tear holes in my hands and my feet
16c and lay me in the dust of death.

18 I can count every one of my bones.
These people stare at me and gloat;
19 they divide my clothing among them.
They cast lots for my robe.

20 O Lord, do not leave me alone,
my strength, make haste to help me!
21 Rescue my soul from the sword,
my life from the grip of these dogs.
22 Save my life from the jaws of these lions,
my poor soul from the horns of these oxen.

23 I will tell of your name to my brethren
and praise you where they are assembled.
24 "You who fear the Lord give him praise;
all sons of Jacob, give him glory.
Revere him, Israel's sons.

25 For he has never despised
nor scorned the poverty of the poor.
From him he has not hidden his face,
but he heard the poor man when he cried."

26 You are my praise in the great assembly.
My vows I will pay before those who fear him.
27 The poor shall eat and shall have their fill.
They shall praise the Lord, those who seek him.
May their hearts live for ever and ever!

28 All the earth shall remember and return to the Lord,
all families of the nations worship before him
29 for the kingdom is the Lord's; he is ruler of the nations.
30 They shall worship him, all the mighty of the earth;
before him shall bow all who go down to the dust.

And my soul shall live for him, 31 my children serve
  him.
They shall tell of the Lord to generations yet to come,
32 declare his faithfulness to peoples yet unborn:
  "These things the Lord has done."

God, shepherd and host:
a psalm of confidence

1 The Lord is my shepherd;
  there is nothing I shall want.
2 Fresh and green are the pastures
  where he gives me repose.
  Near restful waters he leads me,
3 to revive my drooping spirit.

  He guides me along the right path;
  he is true to his name.
4 If I should walk in the valley of darkness
  no evil would I fear.
  You are there with your crook and your staff;
  with these you give me comfort.

5 You have prepared a banquet for me
  in the sight of my foes.
  My head you have anointed with oil;
  my cup is overflowing.

6 Surely goodness and kindness shall follow me
  all the days of my life.
  In the Lord's own house shall I dwell
  for ever and ever.

23

The ruler of the universe
enters his chosen dwelling place

1 The Lord's is the earth and its fullness,
  the world and all its peoples.
2 It is he who set it on the seas;
  on the waters he made it firm.

3 Who shall climb the mountain of the Lord?
  Who shall stand in his holy place?
4 The man with clean hands and pure heart,
  who desires not worthless things,
  (who has not sworn so as to deceive his neighbour.

5 He shall receive blessings from the Lord
  and reward from the God who saves him.
6 Such are the men who seek him,
  seek the face of the God of Jacob.

*   *   *

7 O gates, lift high your heads;
  grow higher, ancient doors.
  Let him enter, the king of glory!

8 Who is the king of glory?
  The Lord, the mighty, the valiant,
  the Lord, the valiant in war.

9 O gates, lift high your heads;
  grow higher, ancient doors.
  Let him enter, the king of glory!

10 Who is he, the king of glory?
  He, the Lord of armies,
  he is the king of glory.

24

Prayer for protection and forgiveness:
an alphabetical psalm

1 To you, O Lord, I lift up my soul.
2 I trust you, let me not be disappointed;
   do not let my enemies triumph.
3 Those who hope in you shall not be disappointed,
   but only those who wantonly break faith.

4 Lord, make me know your ways.
   Lord, teach me your paths.
5 Make me walk in your truth, and teach me:
   for you are God my saviour.

In you I hope all the day long
7c because of your goodness, O Lord.
6 Remember your mercy, Lord,
   and the love you have shown from of old.
7 Do not remember the sins of my youth.
   In your love remember me.

8 The Lord is good and upright.
   He shows the path to those who stray,
9 He guides the humble in the right path;
   he teaches his way to the poor.

10 His ways are faithfulness and love
   for those who keep his covenant and will.
11 Lord, for the sake of your name
   forgive my guilt; for it is great.

12 If anyone fears the Lord
   he will show him the path he should choose.
13 His soul shall live in happiness
   and his children shall possess the land.
14 The Lord's friendship is for those who revere him;
   to them he reveals his covenant.

15 My eyes are always on the Lord;
   for he rescues my feet from the snare.
16 Turn to me and have mercy
   for I am lonely and poor.

17 Relieve the anguish of my heart
   and set me free from my distress.
18 See my affliction and my toil
   and take all my sins away.

19 See how many are my foes;
   how violent their hatred for me.
20 Preserve my life and rescue me.
   Do not disappoint me, you are my refuge.
21 May innocence and uprightness protect me:
   for my hope is in you, O Lord.

22 Redeem Israel, O God, from all its distress.

25

Prayer of a man of integrity

1 Give judgment for me, O Lord:
 for I walk the path of perfection.
 I trust in the Lord; I have not wavered.

2 Examine me, Lord, and try me;
 O test my heart and my mind,
3 for your love is before my eyes
 and I walk according to your truth.

4 I never take my place with liars
 and with hypocrites I shall not go.
5 I hate the evil-doer's company:
 I will not take my place with the wicked.

6 To prove my innocence I wash my hands
 and take my place around your altar,
7 singing a song of thanksgiving,
 proclaiming all your wonders.

8 O Lord, I love the house where you dwell,
 the place where your glory abides.

9 Do not sweep me away with sinners,
 nor my life with bloodthirsty men
10 in whose hands are evil plots,
 whose right hands are filled with gold.

11 As for me, I walk the path of perfection.
 Redeem me and show me your mercy.
12 My foot stands on level ground:
 I will bless the Lord in the assembly.

26

Triumphant trust in God

1 The Lord is my light and my help;
 whom shall I fear?
 The Lord is the stronghold of my life;
 before whom shall I shrink?

2 When evil-doers draw near
 to devour my flesh,
 it is they, my enemies and foes,
 who stumble and fall.

3 Though an army encamp against me
 my heart would not fear.
 Though war break out against me
 even then would I trust.

4 There is one thing I ask of the Lord,
 for this I long,
 to live in the house of the Lord,
 all the days of my life,
 to savour the sweetness of the Lord,
 to behold his temple.

5 For there he keeps me safe in his tent
 in the day of evil.
 He hides me in the shelter of his tent,
 on a rock he sets me safe.

6 And now my head shall be raised
 above my foes who surround me
 and I shall offer within his tent
 a sacrifice of joy.

 I will sing and make music for the Lord

7 O Lord, hear my voice when I call;
 have mercy and answer.
8 Of you my heart has spoken:
 "Seek his face."

It is your face, O Lord, that I seek;
9 hide not your face.
Dismiss not your servant in anger;
you have been my help.

Do not abandon or forsake me,
O God my help!
10 Though father and mother forsake me,
the Lord will receive me.

11 Instruct me, Lord, in your way;
on an even path lead me.
When they lie in ambush 12 protect me
from my enemy's greed.
False witnesses rise against me,
breathing out fury.

13 I am sure I shall see the Lord's goodness
in the land of the living.
14 Hope in him, hold firm and take heart.
Hope in the Lord!

27

Prayer in time of danger

1 To you, O Lord, I call,
   my rock, hear me.
   If you do not heed I shall become
   like those in the grave.

2 Hear the voice of my pleading
   as I call for help,
   as I lift up my hands in prayer
   to your holy place.

3 Do not drag me away with the wicked,
   with the evil-doers,
   who speak words of peace to their neighbours
   but with evil in their hearts.

4 Repay them as their actions deserve
   and the malice of their deeds.
   Repay them for the work of their hands;
   give them their deserts.
5 For they ignore the deeds of the Lord
   and the work of his hands.
   (May he ruin them and never rebuild them.)

6 Blessed be the Lord for he has heard
   my cry, my appeal.
7 The Lord is my strength and my shield;
   in him my heart trusts.
   I was helped, my heart rejoices
   and I praise him with my song.

8 The Lord is the strength of his people,
   the stronghold where his anointed find salvation.
9 Save your people; bless Israel your heritage.
   Be their shepherd and carry them for ever.

28

God's power seen in the storm

1 O give the Lord you sons of God,
   give the Lord glory and power;
2 give the Lord the glory of his name.
   Adore the Lord in his holy court.

3 The Lord's voice resounding on the waters,
   the Lord on the immensity of waters;
4 the voice of the Lord, full of power,
   the voice of the Lord, full of splendour.

5 The Lord's voice shattering the cedars,
   the Lord shatters the cedars of Lebanon;
6 he makes Lebanon leap like a calf
   and Sirion like a young wild-ox.

7 (The Lord's voice flashes flames of fire.)

8 The Lord's voice shaking the wilderness,
   the Lord shakes the wilderness of Kadesh;
9 the Lord's voice rending the oak tree
   and stripping the forest bare.

3b The God of glory thunders.
10 In his temple they all cry: "Glory!"
   The Lord sat enthroned over the flood;
   the Lord sits as king for ever.

11 The Lord will give strength to his people,
   the Lord will bless his people with peace.

29

Thanksgiving for recovery from sickness

2 I will praise you, Lord, you have rescued me
  and have not let my enemies rejoice over me.

*   *   *

3 O Lord, I cried to you for help
  and you, my God, have healed me.
4 O Lord, you have raised my soul from the dead,
  restored me to life from those who sink into the grave.

5 Sing psalms to the Lord, you who love him,
  give thanks to his holy name.
6 His anger lasts but a moment; his favour through life.
  At night there are tears, but joy comes with dawn.

7 I said to myself in my good fortune:
  "Nothing will ever disturb me."
8 Your favour had set me on a mountain fastness,
  then you hid your face and I was put to confusion.

9 To you, Lord, I cried,
  to my God I made appeal:
10 "What profit would my death be, my going to the
   grave?
   Can dust give you praise or proclaim your truth?"

11 The Lord listened and had pity.
   The Lord came to my help.
12 For me you have changed my mourning into dancing,
   you removed my sackcloth and girdled me with joy.
13 So my soul sings psalms to you unceasingly.
   O Lord my God, I will thank you for ever.

30

Confident prayer in distress

2 In you, O Lord, I take refuge.
  Let me never be put to shame.
  In your justice, set me free,
3 hear me and speedily rescue me.

  Be a rock of refuge for me,
  a mighty stronghold to save me,
4 for you are my rock, my stronghold.
  For your name's sake, lead me and guide me.

5 Release me from the snares they have hidden
  for you are my refuge, Lord.
6 Into your hands I commend my spirit.
  It is you who will redeem me, Lord.

  O God of truth, 7 you detest
  those who worship false and empty gods.
8 As for me, I trust in the Lord :
  let me be glad and rejoice in your love.

  You who have seen my affliction
  and taken heed of my soul's distress,
9 have not handed me over to the enemy,
  but set my feet at large.

                *   *   *

10 Have mercy on me, O Lord,
   for I am in distress.
   Tears have wasted my eyes,
   my throat and my heart.

11 For my life is spent with sorrow
   and my years with sighs.
   Affliction has broken down my strength
   and my bones waste away.

12 In the face of all my foes
I am a reproach,
an object of scorn to my neighbours
and of fear to my friends.

Those who see me in the street
run far away from me.
13 I am like a dead man, forgotten in men's hearts,
like a thing thrown away.

14 I have heard the slander of the crowd
fear is all around me,
as they plot together against me,
as they plan to take my life.

15 But as for me, I trust in you, Lord,
I say: "You are my God.
16 My life is in your hands, deliver me
from the hands of those who hate me.

17 Let your face shine on your servant.
Save me in your love.
18 Let me not be put to shame for I call you,
but let the wicked be put to shame!

Let them be silenced in the grave,
19 let lying lips be dumb,
that speak haughtily against the just
with pride and contempt."

*   *   *

20 How great is the goodness, Lord,
that you keep for those who fear you,
that you show to those who trust you
in the sight of men.

21 You hide them in the shelter of your presence
from the plotting of men:
you keep them safe within your tent
from disputing tongues.

22 Blessed be the Lord who has shown me
the wonders of his love
in a fortified city.

23 " I am far removed from your sight "
I said in my alarm.
Yet you heard the voice of my plea
when I cried for help.

24 Love the Lord, all you saints.
He guards his faithful
but the Lord will repay to the full
those who act with pride.

25 Be strong, let your heart take courage.
all who hope in the Lord.

3 1

The joy of being forgiven:
second psalm of repentance

1 Happy the man whose offence is forgiven,
  whose sin is remitted.
2 O happy the man to whom the Lord
  imputes no guilt,
  in whose spirit is no guile.

3 I kept it secret and my frame was wasted
  I groaned all the day long
4 for night and day your hand
  was heavy upon me.
  Indeed, my strength was dried up
  as by the summer's heat.

5 But now I have acknowledged my sins;
  my guilt I did not hide.
  I said: " I will confess
  my offence to the Lord."
  And you, Lord, have forgiven
  the guilt of my sin.

6 So let every good man pray to you
  in the time of need.
  The floods of water may reach high
  but him they shall not reach.
7 You are my hiding place, O Lord;
  you save me from distress.
  (You surround me with cries of deliverance.)

*   *   *

8 I will instruct you and teach you
  the way you should go;
  I will give you counsel
  with my eye upon you.

9 Be not like horse and mule, unintelligent,
  needing bridle and bit,
  else they will not approach you.
10 Many sorrows has the wicked
  but he who trusts in the Lord,
  loving mercy surrounds him.

          *   *   *

11 Rejoice, rejoice in the Lord,
  exult, you just!
  O come, ring out your joy,
  all you upright of heart.

32

Joyful song to the Creator:
national hymn of thanksgiving

1 Ring out your joy to the Lord, O you just;
  for praise is fitting for loyal hearts.

2 Give thanks to the Lord upon the harp,
  with a ten-stringed lute sing him songs.
3 O sing him a song that is new,
  play loudly, with all your skill.

4 For the word of the Lord is faithful
  and all his works to be trusted.
5 The Lord loves justice and right
  and fills the earth with his love.

6 By his word the heavens were made,
  by the breath of his mouth all the stars.
7 He collects the waves of the ocean;
  he stores up the depths of the sea.

8 Let all the earth fear the Lord,
  all who live in the world revere him.
9 He spoke; and it came to be.
  He commanded; it sprang into being.

10 He frustrates the designs of the nations,
  he defeats the plans of the peoples.
11 His own designs shall stand for ever,
  the plans of his heart from age to age.

12 They are happy, whose God is the Lord,
  the people he has chosen as his own.
13 From the heavens the Lord looks forth,
  he sees all the children of men.

14 From the place where he dwells he gazes
  on all the dwellers on the earth,
15 he who shapes the hearts of them all
  and considers all their deeds.

16 A king is not saved by his army,
   nor a warrior preserved by his strength.
17 A vain hope for safety is the horse;
   despite its power it cannot save.

18 The Lord looks on those who revere him,
   on those who hope in his love,
19 to rescue their souls from death,
   to keep them alive in famine.

20 Our soul is waiting for the Lord.
   The Lord is our help and our shield.
21 In him do our hearts find joy.
   We trust in his holy name.

22 May your love be upon us, O Lord,
   as we place all our hope in you.

33

Praise and fear of God:
an alphabetical psalm

2 I will bless the Lord at all times,
  his praise always on my lips;
3 in the Lord my soul shall make its boast.
  The humble shall hear and be glad.

4 Glorify the Lord with me.
  Together let us praise his name.
5 I sought the Lord and he answered me;
  from all my terrors he set me free.

6 Look towards him and be radiant;
  let your faces not be abashed.
7 This poor man called; the Lord heard him
  and rescued him from all his distress.

8 The angel of the Lord is encamped
  around those who revere him, to rescue them.
9 Taste and see that the Lord is good.
  He is happy who seeks refuge in him.

10 Revere the Lord, you his saints.
  They lack nothing, those who revere him.
11 Strong lions suffer want and go hungry
  but those who seek the Lord lack no blessing.

12 Come, children, and hear me
  that I may teach you the fear of the Lord
13 Who is he who longs for life
  and many days, to enjoy his prosperity?

14 Then keep your tongue from evil
  and your lips from speaking deceit.
15 Turn aside from evil and do good;
  seek and strive after peace.

16 The Lord turns his face against the wicked
   to destroy their remembrance from the earth.
17 The Lord turns his eyes to the just
   and his ears to their appeal.

18 They call and the Lord hears
   and rescues them in all their distress.
19 The Lord is close to the broken-hearted;
   those whose spirit is crushed he will save

20 Many are the trials of the just man
   but from them all the Lord will rescue him
21 He will keep guard over all his bones,
   not one of his bones shall be broken.

22 Evil brings death to the wicked;
   those who hate the good are doomed.
23 The Lord ransoms the souls of his servants.
   Those who hide in him shall not be condemned

34

Appeal for vindication

1 O Lord, plead my cause against my foes;
  fight those who fight me.
2 Take up your buckler and shield;
  arise to help me.

3 Take up the javelin and the spear
  against those who pursue me.
  O Lord, say to my soul:
  "I am your salvation."

4 Let those who seek my life
  be shamed and disgraced.
  Let those who plan evil against me
  be routed in confusion.

5 Let them be like chaff before the wind;
  let God's angel scatter them.
6 Let their path be slippery and dark;
  let God's angel pursue them.

7 They have hidden a net for me wantonly;
  they have dug a pit.
8 Let ruin fall upon them
  and take them by surprise.
  Let them be caught in the net they have hidden;
  let them fall into their pit.

9 But my soul shall be joyful in the Lord
  and rejoice in his salvation.
10 My whole being will say:
  "Lord, who is like you
  who rescue the weak from the strong
  and the poor from the oppressor?"

11 Lying witnesses arise
  and accuse me unjustly.
12 They repay me evil for good:
  my soul is forlorn.

13 When they were sick I went into mourning,
   afflicted with fasting.
   My prayer was ever on my lips,
14 as though for a brother, a friend.
   I went as though mourning a mother,
   bowed down with grief.

15 Now that I am in trouble they gather,
   they gather and mock me.
   They take me by surprise and strike me
   and tear me to pieces.
16 They provoke me with mockery on mockery
   and gnash their teeth.

17 O Lord, how long will you look on?
   Come to my rescue!
   Save my life from these raging beasts,
   my soul from these lions.
18 I will thank you in the great assembly
   and praise you amid the throng.

19 Do not let my lying foes
   rejoice over me.
   Do not let those who hate me unjustly
   wink eyes at each other.

20 They wish no peace to the peaceful
   who live in the land.
   They make deceitful plots
21 and with mouths wide open
   their cry against me is: "Yes!
   We saw you do it!"

22 O Lord, you have seen, do not be silent,
   do not stand afar off!
23 Awake, stir to my defence,
   to my cause, O God!

24 Vindicate me, Lord, in your justice,
   do not let them rejoice.
25 Do not let them think: "Yes! we have won,
   we have brought him to an end!"

26 Let them be shamed and brought to disgrace
   who rejoice at my misfortune.
   Let them be covered with shame and confusion
   who raise themselves against me.

27 Let there be joy for those who love my cause.
   Let them say without end:
   "Great is the Lord who delights
   in the peace of his servant."
28 Then my tongue shall speak of your justice
   and all the day long of your praise.

35

Man's malice: God's goodness

2 Sin speaks to the sinner
in the depths of his heart.
There is no fear of God
before his eyes.

3 He so flatters himself in his mind
that he knows not his guilt.
4 In his mouth are mischief and deceit.
All wisdom is gone.

5 He plots the defeat of goodness
as he lies on his bed.
He has set his foot on evil ways,
he clings to what is evil.

*   *   *

6 Your love, Lord, reaches to heaven;
your truth to the skies.
7 Your justice is like God's mountain,
your judgments like the deep.

To both man and beast you give protection.
O Lord, 8 how precious is your love.
My God, the sons of men
find refuge in the shelter of your wings.

9 They feast on the riches of your house;
they drink from the stream of your delight.
10 In you is the source of life
and in your light we see light.

11 Keep on loving those who know you,
doing justice for upright hearts.
12 Let the foot of the proud not crush me
nor the hand of the wicked cast me out.

13 See how the evil-doers have fallen!
Flung down, they shall never arise.

36

Reflections on good and evil:
an alphabetical psalm

1 Do not fret because of the wicked;
  do not envy those who do evil:
2 for they wither quickly like grass
  and fade like the green of the fields.

3 If you trust in the Lord and do good,
  then you will live in the land and be secure.
4 If you find your delight in the Lord,
  he will grant your heart's desire.

5 Commit your life to the Lord,
  trust in him and he will act,
6 so that your justice breaks forth like the light,
  your cause like the noon-day sun.

7 Be still before the Lord and wait in patience;
  do not fret at the man who prospers;
  a man who makes evil plots
14c to bring down the needy and the poor.

8 Calm your anger and forget your rage;
  do not fret, it only leads to evil.
9 For those who do evil shall perish;
  the patient shall inherit the land.

10 A little longer—and the wicked shall have gone.
  Look at his place, he is not there.
11 But the humble shall own the land
  and enjoy the fullness of peace.

12 The wicked man plots against the just
  and gnashes his teeth against him;
13 but the Lord laughs at the wicked
  for he sees that his day is at hand.

14 The sword of the wicked is drawn,
    his bow is bent to slaughter the upright.
15 Their sword shall pierce their own hearts
    and their bows shall be broken to pieces.

16 The just man's few possessions
    are better than the wicked man's wealth;
17 for the power of the wicked shall be broken
    and the Lord will support the just.

18 He protects the lives of the upright,
    their heritage will last for ever.
19 They shall not be put to shame in evil days,
    in time of famine their food shall not fail.

20 But all the wicked shall perish
    and all the enemies of the Lord.
    They are like the beauty of the meadows,
    they shall vanish, they shall vanish like smoke.

21 The wicked man borrows and cannot repay,
    but the just man is generous and gives.
22 Those blessed by the Lord shall own the land,
    but those he has cursed shall be destroyed.

23 The Lord guides the steps of a man
    and makes safe the path of one he loves.
24 Though he stumble he shall never fall
    for the Lord holds him by the hand.

25 I was young and now I am old,
    but I have never seen the just man forsaken
    nor his children begging for bread.
26 All the day he is generous and lends
    and his children become a blessing.

27 Then turn away from evil and do good
    and you shall have a home for ever;
28 for the Lord loves justice
    and will never forsake his friends.

    The unjust shall be wiped out for ever
    and the children of the wicked destroyed.
29 The just shall inherit the land;
    there they shall live for ever.

30 The just man's mouth utters wisdom
   and his lips speak what is right;
31 the law of his God is in his heart,
   his steps shall be saved from stumbling.

32 The wicked man watches for the just
   and seeks occasion to kill him.
33 The Lord will not leave him in his power
   nor let him be condemned when he is judged.

34 Then wait for the Lord, keep to his way.
   It is he who will free you from the wicked,
   raise you up to possess the land
   and see the wicked destroyed.

35 I have seen the wicked triumphant,
   towering like a cedar of Lebanon.
36 I passed by again; he was gone.
   I searched; he was nowhere to be found.

37 See the just man, mark the upright,
   for the man of peace a future lies in store,
38 but sinners shall all be destroyed.
   No future lies in store for the wicked.

39 The salvation of the just comes from the Lord,
   their stronghold in time of distress.
40 The Lord helps them and delivers them
   and saves them : for their refuge is in him.

37

Acknowledgement of guilt:

third psalm of repentance

2 O Lord, do not rebuke me in your anger;
  do not punish me, Lord, in your rage.
3 Your arrows have sunk deep in me;
  your hand has come down upon me.
4 Through your anger all my body is sick:
  through my sin, there is no health in my limbs.

5 My guilt towers higher than my head;
  it is a weight too heavy to bear.
6 My wounds are foul and festering,
  the result of my own folly.
7 I am bowed and brought to my knees.
  I go mourning all the day long.

8 All my frame burns with fever;
  all my body is sick.
9 Spent and utterly crushed,
  I cry aloud in anguish of heart.

10 O Lord, you know all my longing:
  my groans are not hidden from you.
11 My heart throbs, my strength is spent;
  the very light has gone from my eyes.

12 My friends avoid me like a leper;
  those closest to me stand afar off.
13 Those who plot against my life lay snares;
  those who seek my ruin speak of harm,
  planning treachery all the day long.

14 But I am like a deaf man who cannot hear,
  like a dumb man who cannot open his mouth.
15 I am like a man who hears nothing
  in whose mouth is no defence.

16 I count on you, O Lord :
    it is you, Lord God, who will answer.
17 I pray : " Do not let them mock me,
    those who triumph if my foot should slip."

18 For I am on the point of falling
    and my pain is always before me.
19 I confess that I am guilty
    and my sin fills me with dismay.

20 My wanton enemies are numberless
    and my lying foes are many.
21 They repay me evil for good
    and attack me for seeking what is right.

22 O Lord, do not forsake me!
    My God, do not stay afar off!
23 Make haste and come to my help,
    O Lord, my God, my saviour!

38

No abiding city

2 I said: "I will be watchful of my ways
   for fear I should sin with my tongue.
   I will put a curb on my lips
   when the wicked man stands before me."
3 I was dumb, silent and still.
   His prosperity stirred my grief.

4 My heart was burning within me.
   At the thought of it, the fire blazed up
   and my tongue burst into speech:
5 "O Lord, you have shown me my end,
   how short is the length of my days.
   Now I know how fleeting is my life.

6 You have given me a short span of days;
   my life is as nothing in your sight.
   A mere breath, the man who stood so firm,
7 a mere shadow, the man passing by,
   a mere breath the riches he hoards,
   not knowing who will have them."

8 And now, Lord, what is there to wait for?
   In you rests all my hope.
9 Set me free from all my sins,
   do not make me the taunt of the fool.
10 I was silent, not opening my lips,
   because this was all your doing.

11 Take away your scourge from me.
   I am crushed by the blows of your hand.
12 You punish man's sins and correct him;
   like the moth you devour all he treasures.
   Mortal man is no more than a breath;
13 O Lord, hear my prayer.

O Lord, turn your ear to my cry.
Do not be deaf to my tears.
In your house I am a passing guest,
a pilgrim, like all my fathers.
14 Look away that I may breathe again
before I depart to be no more.

39

Thanksgiving and further plea for help

2 I waited, I waited for the Lord
and he stooped down to me;
he heard my cry.

3 He drew me from the deadly pit,
from the miry clay.
He set my feet upon a rock
and made my footsteps firm.

4 He put a new song into my mouth,
praise of our God.
Many shall see and fear
and shall trust in the Lord.

5 Happy the man who has placed
his trust in the Lord
and has not gone over to the rebels
who follow false gods.

6 How many, O Lord my God,
are the wonders and designs
that you have worked for us;
you have no equal.
Should I proclaim and speak of them,
they are more than I can tell!

7 You do not ask for sacrifice and offerings,
but an open ear.
You do not ask for holocaust and victim.
8 Instead, here am I.

In the scroll of the book it stands written
9 that I should do your will.
My God, I delight in your law
in the depth of my heart.

10 Your justice I have proclaimed
in the great assembly.
My lips I have not sealed;
you know it, O Lord.

11 I have not hidden your justice in my heart
but declared your faithful help.
I have not hidden your love and your truth
from the great assembly.

12 O Lord, you will not withhold
your compassion from me.
Your merciful love and your truth
will always guard me.

13 For I am beset with evils
too many to be counted.
My sins have fallen upon me
and my sight fails me.
They are more than the hairs of my head
and my heart sinks.

14 O Lord, come to my rescue,
Lord, come to my aid.
15 O let there be shame and confusion
on those who seek my life.

O let them turn back in confusion,
who delight in my harm.
16 Let them be appalled, covered with shame,
who jeer at my lot.

17 O let there be rejoicing and gladness
for all who seek you.
Let them ever say : " The Lord is great ",
who love your saving help.

18 As for me, wretched and poor,
the Lord thinks of me.
You are my rescuer, my help,
O God, do not delay.

40

Prayer in sickness and betrayal

2 Happy the man who considers the poor and the weak.
  The Lord will save him in the day of evil,
3 will guard him, give him life, make him happy in the
     land
  and will not give him up to the will of his foes.
4 The Lord will help him on his bed of pain,
  he will bring him back from sickness to health.

5 As for me, I said: " Lord, have mercy on me,
  heal my soul for I have sinned against you."
6 My foes are speaking evil against me.
  " How long before he dies and his name be forgotten?"
7 They come to visit me and speak empty words,
  their hearts full of malice, they spread it abroad.

8 My enemies whisper together against me.
  They all weigh up the evil which is on me :
9 " Some deadly thing has fastened upon him,
  he will not rise again from where he lies."
10 Thus even my friend, in whom I trusted,
  who ate my bread, has turned against me.

11 But you, O Lord, have mercy on me.
  Let me rise once more and I will repay them.
12 By this I shall know that you are my friend,
  if my foes do not shout in triumph over me.
13 If you uphold me I shall be unharmed
  and set in your presence for evermore.

*   *   *

14 Blessed be the Lord, the God of Israel
  from age to age. Amen. Amen.

4¹

The exile's nostalgia for God's temple

2 Like the deer that yearns
for running streams,
so my soul is yearning
for you, my God.

3 My soul is thirsting for God,
the God of my life;
when can I enter and see
the face of God?

4 My tears have become my bread,
by night, by day,
as I hear it said all the day long:
"Where is your God?"

5 These things will I remember
as I pour out my soul:
how I would lead the rejoicing crowd
into the house of God,
amid cries of gladness and thanksgiving,
the throng wild with joy.

6 Why are you cast down, my soul,
why groan within me?
Hope in God; I will praise him still,
my saviour and my God.

7 My soul is cast down within me
as I think of you,
from the country of Jordan and Mount Hermon,
from the Hill of Mizar.

8 Deep is calling on deep,
in the roar of waters:
your torrents and all your waves
swept over me.

9 By day the Lord will send
   his loving kindness;
   by night I will sing to him,
   praise the God of my life.

10 I will say to God, my rock:
   " Why have you forgotten me?
   Why do I go mourning
   oppressed by the foe?"

11 With cries that pierce me to the heart,
   my enemies revile me,
   saying to me all the day long:
   " Where is your God?"

12 Why are you cast down, my soul,
   why groan within me?
   Hope in God; I will praise him still,
   my saviour and my God.

42

Longing for God's dwelling place

1 Defend me, O God, and plead my cause
  against a godless nation.
  From deceitful and cunning men
  rescue me, O God.

2 Since you, O God, are my stronghold,
  why have you rejected me?
  Why do I go mourning
  oppressed by the foe?

3 O send forth your light and your truth;
  let these be my guide.
  Let them bring me to your holy mountain
  to the place where you dwell.

4 And I will come to the altar of God,
  the God of my joy.
  My redeemer, I will thank you on the harp,
  O God, my God.

5 Why are you cast down, my soul,
  why groan within me?
  Hope in God; I will praise him still,
  my saviour and my God.

43

God's people in time of disaster:
a national lament

2 We heard with our own ears, O God,
  our fathers have told us the story
  of the things you did in their days,
  you yourself, in days long ago.

3 To plant them you uprooted the nations:
  to let them spread you laid peoples low.
4 No sword of their own won the land;
  no arm of their own brought them victory.
  It was your right hand, your arm
  and the light of your face: for you loved them.

5 It is you, my king, my God,
  who granted victories to Jacob.
6 Through you we beat down our foes;
  in your name we trampled our aggressors.

7 For it was not in my bow that I trusted
  nor yet was I saved by my sword:
8 it was you who saved us from our foes,
  it was you who put our foes to shame.
9 All the day long our boast was in God
  and we praised your name without ceasing.

10 Yet now you have rejected us, disgraced us:
  you no longer go forth with our armies.
11 You make us retreat from the foe
  and our enemies plunder us at will.

12 You make us like sheep for the slaughter
  and scatter us among the nations.
13 You sell your own people for nothing
  and make no profit by the sale.

14 You make us the taunt of our neighbours,
   the mockery and scorn of all who are near.
15 Among the nations, you make us a byword,
   among the peoples a thing of derision.

16 All the day long my disgrace is before me:
   my face is covered with shame
17 at the voice of the taunter, the scoffer,
   at the sight of the foe and avenger.

* * *

18 This befell us though we had not forgotten you
   though we had not been false to your covenant,
19 though we had not withdrawn our hearts;
   though our feet had not strayed from your path
20 Yet you have crushed us in a place of sorrows
   and covered us with the shadow of death.

21 Had we forgotten the name of our God
   or stretched out our hands to another god
22 would not God have found this out,
   he who knows the secrets of the heart?
23 It is for you that we face death all the day long
   and are counted as sheep for the slaughter.

24 Awake, O Lord, why do you sleep?
   Arise, do not reject us for ever!
25 Why do you hide your face
   and forget our oppression and misery?

26 For we are brought down low to the dust;
   our body lies prostrate on the earth.
27 Stand up and come to our help!
   Redeem us because of your love!

44

Royal wedding song

2 My heart overflows with noble words.
To the king I must speak the song I have made;
my tongue as nimble as the pen of a scribe.

* * *

3 You are the fairest of the children of men
and graciousness is poured upon your lips :
because God has blessed you for evermore.

4 O mighty one, gird your sword upon your thigh;
in splendour and state, 5 ride on in triumph
for the cause of truth and goodness and right.

Take aim with your bow in your dread right hand.
6 Your arrows are sharp : peoples fall beneath you
The foes of the king fall down and lose heart.

7 Your throne, O God, shall endure for ever.
A sceptre of justice is the sceptre of your kingdom
8 Your love is for justice; your hatred for evil.

Therefore God, your God, has anointed you
with the oil of gladness above other kings :
9 your robes are fragrant with aloes and myrrh.

From the ivory palace you are greeted with music.
10 The daughters of kings are among your loved ones.
On your right stands the queen in gold of Ophir.

* * *

11 Listen, O daughter, give ear to my words :
forget your own people and your father's house.
12 So will the king desire your beauty :
He is your lord, pay homage to him.

13 And the people of Tyre shall come with gifts,
   the richest of the people shall seek your favour.
14 The daughter of the king is clothed with splendour,
   her robes embroidered with pearls set in gold.

15 She is led to the king with her maiden companions.
16 They are escorted amid gladness and joy;
   they pass within the palace of the king.

*   *   *

17 Sons shall be yours in place of your fathers:
   you will make them princes over all the earth.
18 May this song make your name for ever remembered.
   May the peoples praise you from age to age.

45

Boundless trust in God's power

2 God is for us a refuge and strength,
   a helper close at hand, in time of distress:
3 so we shall not fear though the earth should rock,
   though the mountains fall into the depths of the sea,
4 even though its waters rage and foam,
   even though the mountains be shaken by its waves.

   The Lord of hosts is with us:
   the God of Jacob is our stronghold.

5 The waters of a river give joy to God's city,
   the holy place where the Most High dwells.
6 God is within, it cannot be shaken;
   God will help it at the dawning of the day.
7 Nations are in tumult, kingdoms are shaken:
   he lifts his voice, the earth shrinks away.

8 The Lord of hosts is with us:
   the God of Jacob is our stronghold.

9 Come, consider the works of the Lord
   the redoubtable deeds he has done on the earth.
10 He puts an end to wars over all the earth;
    the bow he breaks, the spear he snaps.
    He burns the shields with fire.
11 " Be still and know that I am God,
    supreme among the nations, supreme on the earth!"

12 The Lord of hosts is with us:
    the God of Jacob is our stronghold.

46

To God, king of the world

2 All peoples, clap your hands,
cry to God with shouts of joy!
3 For the Lord, the Most High, we must fear,
great king over all the earth.

4 He subdues peoples under us
and nations under our feet.
5 Our inheritance, our glory, is from him
given to Jacob out of love.

6 God goes up with shouts of joy;
the Lord goes up with trumpet blast.
7 Sing praise for God, sing praise,
sing praise to our king, sing praise.

8 God is king of all the earth.
Sing praise with all your skill.
9 God is king over the nations;
God reigns on his holy throne.

10 The princes of the peoples are assembled
with the people of Abraham's God.
The rulers of the earth belong to God,
to God who reigns over all.

47

The invincible city of God

2 The Lord is great and worthy to be praised
  in the city of our God.
  His holy mountain 3 rises in beauty,
  the joy of all the earth.

  Mount Sion, true pole of the earth,
  the Great King's city!
4 God, in the midst of its citadels,
  has shown himself its stronghold.

5 For the kings assembled together,
  together they advanced.
6 They saw; at once they were astounded;
  dismayed, they fled in fear.

7 A trembling seized them there,
  like the pangs of birth,
8 or as the east wind destroys
  the ships of Tarshish.

9 As we have heard, so we have seen
  in the city of our God,
  in the city of the Lord of hosts
  which God upholds for ever.

10 O God, we ponder your love
  within your temple.
11 Your praise, O God, like your name
  reaches to the ends of the earth.

  With justice your right hand is filled.
12 Mount Sion rejoices;
  the people of Judah rejoice
  at the sight of your judgments.

13 Walk through Sion, walk all round it;
   count the number of its towers.
14 Review all its ramparts,
   examine its castles,

   that you may tell the next generation
15 that such is our God,
   our God for ever and always.
   It is he who leads us.

48

The problem of justice, pain and death

2 Hear this, all you peoples,
   give heed, all who dwell in the world,
3 men both low and high,
   rich and poor alike!

4 My lips will speak words of wisdom.
   My heart is full of insight.
5 I will turn my mind to a parable,
   with the harp I will solve my problem.

*   *   *

6 Why should I fear in evil days
   the malice of the foes who surround me,
7 men who trust in their wealth,
   and boast of the vastness of their riches?

8 For no man can buy his own ransom,
   or pay a price to God for his life.
9 The ransom of his soul is beyond him.
10 He cannot buy life without end,
    nor avoid coming to the grave.

11 He knows that wise men and fools must both perish
    and leave their wealth to others.
12 Their graves are their homes for ever,
    their dwelling place from age to age,
    though their names spread wide through the land.

13 In his riches, man lacks wisdom:
    he is like the beasts that are destroyed.

*   *   *

14 This is the lot of the self-confident,
    who have others at their beck and call.
15 Like sheep they are driven to the grave,
    where death shall be their shepherd
    and the just shall become their rulers.

With the morning their outward show vanishes
and the grave becomes their home.
16 But God will ransom me from death
and take my soul to himself.

17 Then do not fear when a man grows rich,
when the glory of his house increases.
18 He takes nothing with him when he dies,
his glory does not follow him below.

19 Though he flattered himself while he lived:
"Men will praise me for doing well for myself,"
20 yet he will go to join his fathers,
who will never see the light any more.

21 In his riches, man lacks wisdom:
he is like the beasts that are destroyed.

49

God's judgment on formalism

1 The God of gods, the Lord,
  has spoken and summoned the earth,
  from the rising of the sun to its setting.
2 Out of Sion's perfect beauty he shines.

3 (Our God comes, he keeps silence no longer.)

  Before him fire devours,
  around him tempest rages.
4 He calls on the heavens and the earth
  to witness his judgment of his people.

5 "Summon before me my people
  who made covenant with me by sacrifice."
6 The heavens proclaim his justice,
  for he, God, is the judge.

7 "Listen, my people, I will speak;
  Israel, I will testify against you,
  for I am God your God.
21c I accuse you, lay the charge before you.

8 I find no fault with your sacrifices,
  your offerings are always before me.
9 I do not ask more bullocks from your farms,
  nor goats from among your herds.

10 For I own all the beasts of the forest,
  beasts in their thousands on my hills.
11 I know all the birds in the sky,
  all that moves in the field belong to me

12 Were I hungry, I would not tell you,
  for I own the world and all it holds.
13 Do you think I eat the flesh of bulls,
  or drink the blood of goats?

14 Pay your sacrifice of thanksgiving to God
  and render him your votive offerings.
15 Call on me in the day of distress.
  I will free you and you shall honour me."

16 (But God says to the wicked :)

  "But how can you recite my commandments
  and take my covenant on your lips,
17 you who despise my law
  and throw my words to the winds,

18 you who see a thief and go with him;
  who throw in your lot with adulterers,
19 who unbridle your mouth for evil
  and whose tongue is plotting crime,

20 you who sit and malign your brother
  and slander your own mother's son.
21 You do this, and should I keep silence?
  Do you think that I am like you?

22 Mark this, you who never think of God,
  lest I seize you and you cannot escape;
23 a sacrifice of thanksgiving honours me
  and I will show God's salvation to the upright."

50

Prayer of contrition:
fourth psalm of repentance

3 Have mercy on me, God, in your kindness.
  In your compassion blot out my offence.
4 O wash me more and more from my guilt
  and cleanse me from my sin.

5 My offences truly I know them;
  my sin is always before me.
6 Against you, you alone, have I sinned;
  what is evil in your sight I have done.

  That you may be justified when you give sentence
  and be without reproach when you judge,
7 O see, in guilt I was born,
  a sinner was I conceived.

8 Indeed you love truth in the heart;
  then in the secret of my heart teach me wisdom
9 O purify me, then I shall be clean;
  O wash me, I shall be whiter than snow.

10 Make me hear rejoicing and gladness,
  that the bones you have crushed may thrill.
11 From my sins turn away your face
  and blot out all my guilt.

12 A pure heart create for me, O God,
  put a steadfast spirit within me.
13 Do not cast me away from your presence,
  nor deprive me of your holy spirit.

14 Give me again the joy of your help;
  with a spirit of fervour sustain me,
15 that I may teach transgressors your ways
  and sinners may return to you.

16 O rescue me, God, my helper,
   and my tongue shall ring out your goodness.
17 O Lord, open my lips
   and my mouth shall declare your praise.

18 For in sacrifice you take no delight,
   burnt offering from me you would refuse,
19 my sacrifice, a contrite spirit.
   A humbled, contrite heart you will not spurn.

20 In your goodness, show favour to Sion :
   rebuild the walls of Jerusalem.
21 Then you will be pleased with lawful sacrifice,
   (burnt offerings wholly consumed),
   then you will be offered young bulls on your alter.

5¹

The fate of the deceitful

3 Why do you boast of your wickedness,
  you champion of evil?
4 Why plan ruin all the day long,
  (your tongue like a sharpened razor,)
  you master of deceit.

5 You love evil more than good;
  lies more than truth.
6 You love the destructive word,
  you tongue of deceit.

7 For this God will destroy you
  and remove you for ever.
  He will snatch you from your tent and uproot you
  from the land of the living.

8 The just shall see and fear.
  They shall laugh and say:
9 " So this is the man who refused
  to take God as his stronghold,
  but trusted in the greatness of his wealth
  and grew powerful by his crimes."

10 But I am like a growing olive tree
  in the house of God.
  I trust in the goodness of God
  for ever and ever.

11 I will thank you for evermore;
  for this is your doing.
  I will proclaim that your name is good,
  in the presence of your friends.

52

The fools

2 The fool has said in his heart:
" There is no God above."
Their deeds are corrupt, depraved
not a good man is left.

3 God looks down from heaven
on the sons of men,
to see if any are wise,
if any seek God.

4 All have left the right path;
depraved, every one.
There is not a good man left,
no, not even one.

5 Will the evil-doers not understand?
They eat up my people
as though they ate bread;
they never pray to God.

6 See how they tremble with fear
without cause for fear:
for God scatters the bones of the wicked.
They are shamed, rejected by God.

7 O that Israel's salvation might come from Sion!
When God delivers his people from bondage,
then Jacob will be glad and Israel rejoice.

53

Cry for God's help

3 O God, save me by your name;
   by your power, uphold my cause.
4 O God, hear my prayer;
   listen to the words of my mouth.

5 For proud men have risen against me,
   ruthless men seek my life.
   They have no regard for God.

6 But I have God for my help.
   The Lord upholds my life.
7 Let the evil recoil upon my foes:
   you who are faithful, destroy them.

8 I will sacrifice to you with willing heart
   and praise your name for it is good:
9 for you have rescued me from all my distress
   and my eyes have seen the downfall of my foes.

54

Distress of a man betrayed by his friend

2 O God, listen to my prayer,
  do not hide from my pleading,
3 attend to me and reply;
  with my cares, I cannot rest.

  I tremble 4 at the shouts of the foe,
  at the cries of the wicked;
  for they bring down evil upon me.
  They assail me with fury.

5 My heart is stricken within me,
  death's terror is on me,
6 trembling and fear fall upon me
  and horror overwhelms me.

7 O that I had wings like a dove
  to fly away and be at rest.
8 So I would escape far away
  and take refuge in the desert.

9 I would hasten to find a shelter
  from the raging wind,
  from the destructive storm, O Lord,
10 and from their plotting tongues.

  For I can see nothing but violence
  and strife in the city.
11 Night and day they patrol
  high on the city walls.

  It is full of wickedness and evil;
12 it is full of sin.
  Its streets are never free
  from tyranny and deceit.

13 If this had been done by an enemy
  I could bear his taunts.
  If a rival had risen against me,
  I could hide from him.

14 But it is you, my own companion,
 my intimate friend!
15 (How close was the friendship between us)
 We walked together in harmony
 in the house of God.

16 May death fall suddenly upon them!
 Let them go to the grave:
 for wickedness dwells in their homes
 and deep in their hearts.

17 As for me, I will cry to God
 and the Lord will save me.
18 Evening, morning and at noon
 I will cry and lament.

19 He will deliver my soul in peace
 in the attack against me:
 for those who fight me are many,
18c but he hears my voice.

20 God will hear and will humble them,
 the eternal judge:
 for they will not amend their ways.
 They have no fear of God.

21 The traitor has turned against his friends;
 he has broken his word.
22 His speech is softer than butter,
 but war is in his heart.
 His words are smoother than oil,
 but they are naked swords.

23 Entrust your cares to the Lord
 and he will support you.
 He will never allow
 the just man to stumble.

24 But you, O God, will bring them down
 to the pit of death.
 Deceitful and bloodthirsty men
 shall not live half their days.

 O Lord, I will trust in you.

55

Unshakable confidence in God

2 Have mercy on me, God, men crush me;
   they fight me all day long and oppress me.
3 My foes crush me all the day long,
   for many fight proudly against me.

4 When I fear, I will trust in you,
5 in God whose word I praise.
   In God I trust, I shall not fear:
   what can mortal man do to me?

6 All day long they distort my words,
   all their thought is to harm me.
7 They band together in ambush,
   track me down and seek my life.

8 Repay them, God, for their crimes;
   in your anger, cast down the peoples.
9 You have kept an account of my wanderings;
   you have kept a record of my tears;
   (are they not written in your book?)
10 Then my foes will be put to flight
   on the day that I call to you.

   This I know, that God is on my side.
11 In God, whose word I praise,
   in the Lord, whose word I praise,
12 in God I trust; I shall not fear:
   what can mortal man do to me?

13 I am bound by the vows I have made you.
   O God, I will offer you praise
14 for you rescued my soul from death,
   you kept my feet from stumbling
   that I may walk in the presence of God
   in the light of the living.

56

In time of danger:
a national lament

2 Have mercy on me, God, have mercy
  for in you my soul has taken refuge.
  In the shadow of your wings I take refuge
  till the storms of destruction pass by.

3 I call to God the Most High,
  to God who has always been my help.
4 May he send from heaven and save me
  and shame those who assail me.

  May God send his truth and his love.

5 My soul lies down among lions,
  who would devour the sons of men.
  Their teeth are spears and arrows,
  their tongue a sharpened sword.

6 O God, arise above the heavens;
  may your glory shine on earth!

7 They laid a snare for my steps,
  my soul was bowed down.
  They dug a pit in my path
  but fell in it themselves.

8 My heart is ready, O God,
  my heart is ready.
  I will sing, I will sing your praise.
9 Awake my soul,
  awake lyre and harp,
  I will awake the dawn.

10 I will thank you Lord among the peoples,
   praise you among the nations;
11 for your love reaches to the heavens
   and your truth to the skies.

12 O God, arise above the heavens;
   may your glory shine on earth!

57

Condemnation of injustice

2 Do you truly speak justice, you who hold divine power?
  Do you mete out fair judgment to the sons of men?
3 No, in your hearts you devise injustice;
  your hands deal out violence to the land.

4 In their wickedness they have gone astray from their
    birth :
  they wandered among lies as soon as they were born.
5 Their venom is like the venom of the snake;
  they are heedless as the adder that turns a deaf ear
6 for fear it should hear the snake-charmer's voice,
  the voice of the skilful dealer in spells.

7 O God, break the teeth in their mouths,
  tear out the fangs of these wild beasts, O Lord !
8 Let them vanish like water that runs away :
  let them wither like grass that is trodden underfoot :
9 let them be like the snail that dissolves into slime :
  like a woman's miscarriage that never sees the sun.

10 Before they put forth thorns, like a bramble,
   let them be swept away, green wood or dry !
11 The just shall rejoice at the sight of vengeance;
   they shall bathe their feet in the blood of the wicked.
12 "Truly," men shall say, "the just are rewarded.
   Truly, there is a God who does justice on earth."

58

Appeal to God, the stronghold

2 Rescue me, God, from my foes;
   protect me from those who attack me.
3 O rescue me from those who do evil
   and save me from blood-thirsty men.

4 See, they lie in wait for my life;
   powerful men band together against me.
   For no offence, no sin of mine, Lord,
5 for no guilt of mine they rush to take their stand.

   Awake, come to my aid and see!
6 Lord of hosts, you are Israel's God.
   Rouse yourself and punish the nations;
   show no mercy to evil traitors.

7 Each evening they come back like dogs.
   They howl and roam about the city,
   they prowl in search of food,
   they snarl till they have their fill.

8 See how they gabble open-mouthed;
   their lips are filled with insults.
   "For who," they say, "will hear us?"
9 But you, Lord, will laugh them to scorn.
   You make light of all the nations.

10 O my Strength, it is you to whom I turn,
   for you, O God, are my stronghold,
11 the God who shows me love.

   O God, come to my aid
   and let me look in triumph on my foes.
12 God, kill them lest my people be seduced;
   rout them by your power, lay them low.

It is you, O Lord, who are our shield.
13 For the sins of their mouths and their lips,
   for the curses and lies that they speak
   let them be caught in their pride.

14 Destroy them, Lord, in your anger.
   Destroy them till they are no more.
   Let men know that God is the ruler
   over Jacob and the ends of the earth.

15 Each evening they come back like dogs.
   They howl and roam about the city,
16 they prowl in search of food,
   they snarl till they have their fill.

17 As for me, I will sing of your strength
   and each morning acclaim your love
   for you have been my stronghold,
   a refuge in the day of my distress.

18 O my Strength, it is you to whom I turn,
   for you, O God, are my stronghold,
   the God who shows me love.

59

After a defeat

3 O God, you have rejected us and broken us.
You have been angry; come back to us.

4 You have made the earth quake, torn it open
Repair what is shattered for it sways.
5 You have inflicted hardships on your people
and made us drink a wine that dazed us.

6 You have given those who fear you a signal
to flee from the enemy's bow.
7 O come and deliver your friends,
help with your right hand and reply.

* * *

8 From his holy place God has made this promise:
"I will triumph and divide the land of Shechem,
I will measure out the valley of Succoth.

9 Gilead is mine and Manasseh,
Ephraim I take for my helmet,
Judah for my commander's staff.

10 Moab I will use for my washbowl;
on Edom I will plant my shoe.
Over the Philistines I will shout in triumph."

11 But who will lead me to conquer the fortress?
Who will bring me face to face with Edom?
12 Will you utterly reject us, O God,
and no longer march with our armies?

13 Give us help against the foe:
for the help of man is vain.
14 With God we shall do bravely
and he will trample down our foes.

60

Prayer of an exile

2 O God, hear my cry!
  Listen to my prayer!
3 From the end of the earth I call:
  my heart is faint.

  On the rock too high for me to reach
  set me on high,
4 O you who have been my refuge,
  my tower against the foe.

5 Let me dwell in your tent for ever
  and hide in the shelter of your wings.
6 For you, O God, hear my prayer
  and grant me the heritage of those who fear you.

7 May you lengthen the life of the king:
  may his years cover many generations.
8 May he ever sit enthroned before God:
  bid love and truth be his protection.

9 So I will always praise your name
  and day after day fulfil my vows.

61

God, the rock of strength:
a psalm of confidence

2 In God alone is my soul at rest;
   my help comes from him.
3 He alone is my rock, my stronghold,
   my fortress: I stand firm.

4 How long will you all attack one man
   to break him down,
   as though he were a tottering wall,
   or a tumbling fence?

5 Their plan is only to destroy:
   they take pleasure in lies.
   With their mouth they utter blessing
   but in their heart they curse.

6 In God alone be at rest, my soul;
   for my hope comes from him.
7 He alone is my rock, my stronghold,
   my fortress: I stand firm.

8 In God is my safety and glory,
   the rock of my strength.
   Take refuge in God 9 all you people.
   Trust him at all times.
   Pour out your hearts before him
   for God is our refuge.

10 Common folk are only a breath,
   great men an illusion.
   Placed in the scales, they rise;
   they weigh less than a breath.

11 Do not put your trust in oppression
   nor vain hopes on plunder.
   Do not set your heart on riches
   even when they increase.

12 For God has said only one thing:
   only two do I know:
   that to God alone belongs power
13 and to you, Lord, love;
   and that you repay each man
   according to his deeds.

62

Longing for God

2 O God, you are my God, for you I long;
    for you my soul is thirsting.
  My body pines for you
    like a dry, weary land without water.
3 So I gaze on you in the sanctuary
    to see your strength and your glory.

4 For your love is better than life,
    my lips will speak your praise.
5 So I will bless you all my life,
    in your name I will lift up my hands.
6 My soul shall be filled as with a banquet,
    my mouth shall praise you with joy.

7 On my bed I remember you.
  On you I muse through the night
8 for you have been my help;
    in the shadow of your wings I rejoice.
9 My soul clings to you;
    your right hand holds me fast.

10 Those who seek to destroy my life
    shall go down to the depths of the earth.
11 They shall be put into the power of the sword
    and left as the prey of the jackals.
12 But the king shall rejoice in God;
    (all that swear by him shall be blessed)
    for the mouth of liars shall be silenced.

63

The defeat of God's enemies

2 Hear my voice, O God, as I complain,
 guard my life from dread of the foe.
3 Hide me from the band of the wicked,
 from the throng of those who do evil.

4 They sharpen their tongues like swords;
 they aim bitter words like arrows
5 to shoot at the innocent from ambush,
 shooting suddenly and recklessly.

6 They scheme their evil course;
 they conspire to lay secret snares.
 They say: "Who will see us?
7 Who can search out our crimes?"

*   *   *

He will search who searches the mind
 and knows the depths of the heart.
8 God has shot an arrow at them
 and dealt them sudden wounds.
9 Their own tongue has brought them to ruin
 and all who see them mock.

10 Then all men will fear;
 they will tell what God has done.
 They will understand God's deeds.
11 The just will rejoice in the Lord
 and fly to him for refuge.
 All the upright hearts will glory.

64

Song of springtime:
a psalm of worship

2 To you our praise is due
in Sion, O God.
To you we pay our vows,
3 you who hear our prayer.

To you all flesh will come
4 with its burden of sin.
Too heavy for us, our offences,
but you wipe them away.

5 Blessed he whom you choose and call
to dwell in your courts.
We are filled with the blessings of your house,
of your holy temple.

6 You keep your pledge with wonders,
O God our saviour,
the hope of all the earth
and of far distant isles.

7 You uphold the mountains with your strength,
you are girded with power.
8 You still the roaring of the seas,
(the roaring of their waves)
and the tumult of the peoples.

9 The ends of the earth stand in awe
at the sight of your wonders.
The lands of sunrise and sunset
you fill with your joy.

10 You care for the earth, give it water,
you fill it with riches.
Your river in heaven brims over
to provide its grain.

And thus you provide for the earth;
11 You drench its furrows,
   you level it, soften it with showers,
   you bless its growth.

12 You crown the year with your goodness.
   Abundance flows in your steps,
13 in the pastures of the wilderness it flows.

   The hills are girded with joy,
14 the meadows covered with flocks,
   the valleys are decked with wheat.
   They shout for joy, yes, they sing.

65

A people's thanksgiving

1 Cry out with joy to God all the earth,
2 O sing to the glory of his name.
O render him glorious praise.
3 Say to God: "How tremendous your deeds!

Because of the greatness of your strength
your enemies cringe before you.
4 Before you all the earth shall bow;
shall sing to you, sing to your name!"

5 Come and see the works of God,
tremendous his deeds among men.
6 He turned the sea into dry land,
they passed through the river dry-shod

Let our joy then be in him;
7 he rules for ever by his might.
His eyes keep watch over the nations:
let rebels not rise against him.

8 O peoples, bless our God,
let the voice of his praise resound,
9 of the God who gave life to our souls
and kept our feet from stumbling.

10 For you, O God, have tested us,
you have tried us as silver is tried:
11 you led us, God, into the snare;
you laid a heavy burden on our backs.

12 You let men ride over our heads;
we went through fire and through water
but then you brought us relief.

13 Burnt offering I bring to your house;
to you I will pay my vows,
14 the vows which my lips have uttered,
which my mouth spoke in my distress.

15 I will offer burnt offerings of fatlings
    with the smoke of burning rams.
    I will offer bullocks and goats.

16 Come and hear, all who fear God.
    I will tell what he did for my soul:
17 to him I cried aloud,
    with high praise ready on my tongue.

18 If there had been evil in my heart,
    the Lord would not have listened.
19 But truly God has listened;
    he has heeded the voice of my prayer.

20 Blessed be God who did not reject my prayer
    nor withhold his love from me.

66

Harvest song

2 O God, be gracious and bless us
  and let your face shed its light upon us.
3 So will your ways be known upon earth
  and all nations learn your saving help.

4 Let the peoples praise you, O God;
  let all the peoples praise you.

5 Let the nations be glad and exult
  for you rule the world with justice.
  With fairness you rule the peoples,
  you guide the nations on earth.

6 Let the peoples praise you, O God;
  let all the peoples praise you.

7 The earth has yielded its fruit
  for God, our God, has blessed us.
8 May God still give us his blessing
  till the ends of the earth revere him.

Let the peoples praise you, O God;
let all the peoples praise you.

67

The journey of God's people:
triumphant hymn of thanks

2 Let God arise, let his foes be scattered.
Let those who hate him flee before him.
3 As smoke is blown away so will they be blown away;
like wax that melts before the fire,
so the wicked shall perish at the presence of God.

4 But the just shall rejoice at the presence of God,
they shall exult and dance for joy.
5 O sing to the Lord, make music to his name;
make a highway for him who rides on the clouds.
Rejoice in the Lord, exult at his presence.

6 Father of the orphan, defender of the widow,
such is God in his holy place.
7 God gives the lonely a home to live in;
he leads the prisoners forth into freedom:
but rebels must dwell in a parched land.

8 When you went forth, O God, at the head of your
people,
when you marched across the desert, 9 the earth
trembled:
the heavens melted at the presence of God,
at the presence of God, Israel's God.

10 You poured down, O God, a generous rain:
when your people were starved you gave them new
life.
11 It was there that your people found a home,
prepared in your goodness, O God, for the poor.

12 The Lord gives the word to the bearers of good tidings:
" The Almighty has defeated a numberless army
13 and kings and armies are in flight, in flight
while you were at rest among the sheepfolds."

14 At home the women already share the spoil.
They are covered with silver as the wings of a dove,
its feathers brilliant with shining gold
15 and jewels flashing like snow on Mount Zalmon.

16 The mountains of Bashan are mighty mountains;
high-ridged mountains are the mountains of Bashan.
17 Why look with envy, you high-ridged mountains,
at the mountain where God has chosen to dwell?
It is there that the Lord shall dwell for ever.

18 The chariots of God are thousands upon thousand.
The Lord has come from Sinai to the holy place.
19 You have gone up on high; you have taken captives,
receiving men in tribute, O God,
even those who rebel, into your dwelling, O Lord.

20 May the Lord be blessed day after day.
He bears our burdens, God our saviour.
21 This God of ours is a God who saves.
The Lord our God holds the keys of death.
22 And God will smite the head of his foes,
the crown of those who persist in their sins.

23 The Lord said: " I will bring them back from Bashan;
I will bring them back from the depth of the sea.
24 Then your feet will tread in their blood
and the tongues of your dogs take their share of the
foe."

25 They see your solemn procession, O God,
the procession of my God, of my king, to the sanctuary :
26 the singers in the forefront, the musicians coming last,
between them, maidens sounding their timbrels.

27 " In festive gatherings, bless the Lord;
bless God, O you who are Israel's sons."
28 There is Benjamin, least of the tribes, at the head,
Judah's princes, a mighty throng,
Zebulun's princes, Naphtali's princes.

29 Show forth, O God, show forth your might,
your might, O God, which you have shown for us.
30 For the sake of your temple high in Jerusalem
may kings come to you bringing their tribute.

31 Threaten the wild beast that dwells in the reeds,
   the bands of the mighty and lords of the peoples.
   Let them bow down offering silver.
   Scatter the peoples who delight in war.
32 Princes will make their way from Egypt:
   Ethiopia will stretch out her hands to God.

33 Kingdoms of the earth, sing to God, praise the Lord
34 who rides on the heavens, the ancient heavens.
   He thunders his voice, his mighty voice.
35 Come, acknowledge the power of God.

   His glory is over Israel; his might is in the skies.
36 God is to be feared in his holy place.
   He is the Lord, Israel's God.
   He gives strength and power to his people.

   Blessed be God!

68

Cry from the depths of sorrow

2 Save me, O God,
   for the waters have risen to my neck.

3 I have sunk into the mud of the deep
   and there is no foothold.
   I have entered the waters of the deep
   and the waves overwhelm me.

4 I am wearied with all my crying,
   my throat is parched.
   My eyes are wasted away
   from looking for my God.

5 More numerous than the hairs on my head
   are those who hate me without cause.
   Those who attack me with lies
   are too much for my strength.

   How can I restore
   what I have never stolen?
6 O God, you know my sinful folly;
   my sins you can see.

7 Let not those who hope in you be put to shame
   through me, Lord of hosts:
   let not those who seek you be dismayed
   through me, God of Israel.

8 It is for you that I suffer taunts,
   that shame covers my face,
9 that I have become a stranger to my brothers,
   an alien to my own mother's sons.
10 I burn with zeal for your house
   and taunts against you fall on me.

11 When I afflict my soul with fasting
   they make it a taunt against me.
12 When I put on sackcloth in mourning
   then they make me a byword,
13 the gossip of men at the gates,
   the subject of drunkards' songs.

14 This is my prayer to you,
   my prayer for your favour.
   In your great love, answer me, O God,
   with your help that never fails:
15 rescue me from sinking in the mud;
   save me from my foes.

   Save me from the waters of the deep
16 lest the waves overwhelm me.
   Do not let the deep engulf me
   nor death close its mouth on me.

17 Lord, answer, for your love is kind;
   in your compassion, turn towards me.
18 Do not hide your face from your servant;
   answer quickly for I am in distress.
19 Come close to my soul and redeem me;
   ransom me pressed by my foes.

20 You know how they taunt and deride me;
   my oppressors are all before you.
21 Taunts have broken my heart;
   I have reached the end of my strength.
   I looked in vain for compassion,
   for consolers; not one could I find.

22 For food they gave me poison;
   in my thirst they gave me vinegar to drink
23 Let their table be a snare to them
   and their festive banquets a trap.
24 Let their eyes grow dim and blind;
   let their limbs tremble and shake.

25 Pour out your anger upon them,
let the heat of your fury overtake them.
26 Let their camp be left desolate;
let no one dwell in their tents:
27 for they persecute one whom you struck;
they increase the pain of him you wounded.

28 Charge them with guilt upon guilt;
let them never be found just in your sight.
29 Blot them out from the book of the living;
do not enrol them among the just.
30 As for me in my poverty and pain
let your help, O God, lift me up.

31 I will praise God's name with a song;
I will glorify him with thanksgiving.
32 A gift pleasing God more than oxen,
more than beasts prepared for sacrifice.

33 The poor when they see it will be glad
and God-seeking hearts will revive;
34 for the Lord listens to the needy
and does not spurn his servants in their chains.
35 Let the heavens and the earth give him praise,
the sea and all its living creatures.

36 For God will bring help to Sion
and rebuild the cities of Judah
and men shall dwell there in possession.
37 The sons of his servants shall inherit it;
those who love his name shall dwell there.

69

Prayer of trust and appeal

2 O God, make haste to my rescue,
   Lord, come to my aid!
3 Let there be shame and confusion
   on those who seek my life.

   O let them turn back in confusion,
   who delight in my harm,
4 let them retreat, covered with shame,
   who jeer at my lot.

5 Let there be rejoicing and gladness
   for all who seek you.
   Let them say for ever: "God is great,"
   who love your saving help.

6 As for me, wretched and poor,
   come to me, O God.
   You are my rescuer, my help,
   O Lord, do not delay.

70

Prayer in old age

1 In you, O Lord, I take refuge;
   let me never be put to shame.
2 In your justice rescue me, free me :
   pay heed to me and save me.

3 Be a rock where I can take refuge,
   a mighty stronghold to save me;
   for you are my rock, my stronghold.
4 Free me from the hand of the wicked,
   from the grip of the unjust, of the oppressor.

5 It is you, O Lord, who are my hope,
   my trust, O Lord, since my youth.
6 On you I have leaned from my birth,
   from my mother's womb you have been my help.
   My hope has always been in you.

7 My fate has filled many with awe
   but you are my strong refuge.
8 My lips are filled with your praise,
   with your glory all the day long.
9 Do not reject me now that I am old;
   when my strength fails do not forsake me.

10 For my enemies are speaking about me;
   those who watch me take counsel together
11 saying : " God has forsaken him; follow him,
   seize him; there is no one to save him."
12 O God, do not stay far off :
   my God, make haste to help me!

13 Let them be put to shame and destroyed,
   all those who seek my life.
   Let them be covered with shame and confusion,
   all those who seek to harm me.

14 But as for me, I will always hope
and praise you more and more.
15 My lips will tell of your justice
and day by day of your help
(though I can never tell it all).

16 I will declare the Lord's mighty deeds
proclaiming your justice, yours alone.
17 O God, you have taught me from my youth
and I proclaim your wonders still.

18 Now that I am old and grey-headed,
do not forsake me, God.
Let me tell of your power to all ages,
praise your strength 19 and justice to the skies,
tell of you who have worked such wonders.
O God, who is like you?

20 You have burdened me with bitter troubles
but you will give me back my life.
You will raise me from the depths of the earth;
21 you will exalt me and console me again.

22 So I will give you thanks on the lyre
for your faithful love, my God.
To you will I sing with the harp
to you, the Holy One of Israel.
23 When I sing to you my lips shall rejoice
and my soul, which you have redeemed.

24 And all day long my tongue
shall tell the tale of your justice:
for they are put to shame and disgraced,
all those who seek to harm me.

71

The kingdom of peace

1 O God, give your judgment to the king,
  to a king's son your justice,
2 that he may judge your people in justice
  and your poor in right judgment.

3 May the mountains bring forth peace for the people
  and the hills, justice.
4 May he defend the poor of the people
  and save the children of the needy
  (and crush the oppressor).

5 He shall endure like the sun and the moon
  from age to age.
6 He shall descend like rain on the meadow,
  like raindrops on the earth.

7 In his days justice shall flourish
  and peace till the moon fails.
8 He shall rule from sea to sea,
  from the Great River to earth's bounds.

9 Before him his enemies shall fall,
  his foes lick the dust.
10 The kings of Tarshish and the sea coasts
  shall pay him tribute.

  The kings of Sheba and Seba
  shall bring him gifts.
11 Before him all kings shall fall prostrate,
  all nations shall serve him.

12 For he shall save the poor when they cry
  and the needy who are helpless.
13 He will have pity on the weak
  and save the lives of the poor.

14 From oppression he will rescue their lives,
   to him their blood is dear.
15 (Long may he live,
   may the gold of Sheba be given him.)
   They shall pray for him without ceasing
   and bless him all the day.

16 May corn be abundant in the land
   to the peaks of the mountains.
   May its fruit rustle like Lebanon;
   may men flourish in the cities
   like grass on the earth.

17 May his name be blessed for ever
   and endure like the sun.
   Every tribe shall be blessed in him,
   all nations bless his name.

*   *   *

18 Blessed be the Lord, God of Israel,
   who alone works wonders,
19 ever blessed his glorious name.
   Let his glory fill the earth.

Amen! Amen!

72

The problem of innocent suffering

1 How good God is to Israel,
  to those who are pure of heart.
2 Yet my feet came close to stumbling,
  my steps had almost slipped
3 for I was filled with envy of the proud
  when I saw how the wicked prosper.

4 For them there are no pains;
  their bodies are sound and sleek.
5 They have no share in men's sorrows;
  they are not stricken like others.

6 So they wear their pride like a necklace,
  they clothe themselves with violence.
7 Their hearts overflow with malice,
  their minds seethe with plots.

8 They scoff; they speak with malice;
  from on high they plan oppression.
9 They have set their mouths in the heavens
  and their tongues dictate to the earth.

10 So the people turn to follow them
  and drink in all their words.
11 They say: "How can God know?
  Does the Most High take any notice?"
12 Look at them, such are the wicked,
  but untroubled, they grow in wealth.

*   *   *

13 How useless to keep my heart pure
  and wash my hands in innocence,
14 when I was stricken all day long,
  suffered punishment day after day.

15 Then I said: "If I should speak like that,
   I should betray the race of your sons."

16 I strove to fathom this problem,
   too hard for my mind to understand,
17 until I pierced the mysteries of God
   and understand what becomes of the wicked.

*   *   *

18 How slippery the paths on which you set them;
   you make them slide to destruction.
19 How suddenly they come to their ruin,
   wiped out, destroyed by terrors.
20 Like a dream one wakes from, O Lord,
   when you wake you dismiss them as phantoms.

21 And so when my heart grew embittered
   and when I was cut to the quick,
22 I was stupid and did not understand,
   no better than a beast in your sight.

23 Yet I was always in your presence;
   you were holding me by my right hand.
24 You will guide me by your counsel
   and so you will lead me to glory.

25 What else have I in heaven but you?
   Apart from you I want nothing on earth.
26 My body and my heart faint for joy;
   God is my possession for ever.

27 All those who abandon you shall perish;
   you will destroy all those who are faithless.
28 To be near God is my happiness.
   I have made the Lord God my refuge.
   I will tell of all your works
   at the gates of the city of Sion.

73

God's people mourn over the ruined temple:
a national lament

1 Why, O God, have you cast us off for ever?
  Why blaze with anger against the sheep of your
    pasture?
2 Remember your people whom you chose long ago,
  the tribe you redeemed to be your own possession,
  the mountain of Sion where you made your dwelling.

3 Turn your steps to these places that are utterly ruined!
  The enemy has laid waste the whole of the sanctuary.
4 Your foes have made uproar in your house of prayer:
  they have set up their emblems, their foreign emblems,
5 high above the entrance to the sanctuary.

Their axes 6 have battered the wood of its doors.
They have struck together with hatchet and pickaxe.
7 O God, they have set your sanctuary on fire:
  they have razed and profaned the place where you
    dwell.

8 They said in their hearts: "Let us utterly crush them:
  let us burn every shrine of God in the land."
9 There is no sign from God, nor have we a prophet,
  we have no one to tell us how long it will last.

10 How long, O God, is the enemy to scoff?
   Is the foe to insult your name for ever?
11 Why, O Lord, do you hold back your hand?
   Why do you keep your right hand hidden?

12 Yet God is our king from time past,
   the giver of help through all the land.
13 It was you who divided the sea by your might,
   who shattered the heads of the monsters in the sea.

14 It was you who crushed Leviathan's heads
   and gave him as food to the untamed beasts.
15 It was you who opened springs and torrents;
   it was you who dried up ever-flowing rivers.

16 Yours is the day and yours is the night.
   It was you who appointed the light and the sun:
17 it was you who fixed the bounds of the earth:
   you who made both summer and winter.

18 Remember this, Lord, and see the enemy scoffing,
   a senseless people insults your name.
19 Do not give Israel, your dove, to the hawk
   nor forget the life of your poor servants for ever.

20 Remember your covenant; every cave in the land
   is a place where violence makes its home.
21 Do not let the oppressed return disappointed;
   let the poor and the needy bless your name.

22 Arise, O God, and defend your cause!
   Remember how the senseless revile you all the day
23 Do not forget the clamour of your foes,
   the daily increasing uproar of your foes.

74

Judge of the world

2 We give thanks to you, O God,
   we give thanks and call upon your name.
   We recount your wonderful deeds.

* * *

3 "When I reach the appointed time,
   then I will judge with justice.
4 Though the earth and all who dwell in it may rock,
   it is I who uphold its pillars.

5 I say to the boastful : 'Do not boast,'
   to the wicked : 'Do not flaunt your strength
6 do not flaunt your strength on high.
   Do not speak with insolent pride.' "

7 For neither from the east nor from the west,
   nor from desert or mountains comes judgment,
8 but God himself is the judge.
   One he humbles, another he exalts.

9 The Lord holds a cup in his hand,
   full of wine, foaming and spiced.
   He pours it; they drink it to the dregs :
   all the wicked on the earth must drain it.

10 As for me, I will rejoice for ever
   and sing psalms to Jacob's God.
11 He shall break the power of the wicked,
   while the strength of the just shall be exalted.

75

Song after victory

2 God is made known in Judah;
 in Israel his name is great.
3 He set up his tent in Jerusalem
 and his dwelling place in Sion.
4 It was there he broke the flashing arrows,
 the shield, the sword, the armour.

5 You, Lord, are resplendent,
 more majestic than the everlasting mountains.
6 The warriors, despoiled, slept in death;
 the hands of the soldiers were powerless.
7 At your threat, O God of Jacob,
 horse and rider lay stunned.

8 You, you alone, strike terror.
 Who shall stand when your anger is roused?
9 You uttered your sentence from the heavens;
 the earth in terror was still
10 when God arose to judge,
 to save the humble of the earth.

11 Men's anger will serve to praise you;
 its survivors surround you in joy.
12 Make vows to your God and fulfil them.
 Let all pay tribute to him who strikes terror,
13 who cuts short the breath of princes,
 who strikes terror in the kings of the earth.

76

God's dealings with Israel:
prayer of a perplexed man

2 I cry aloud to God,
   cry aloud to God that he may hear me.

3 In the day of my distress I sought the Lord.
   At night my hands were raised without ceasing;
   my soul refused to be consoled.
4 I remembered my God and I groaned.
   I pondered and my spirit fainted.

5 You withheld sleep from my eyes.
   I was troubled, I could not speak.
6 I thought of the days of long ago
   and remembered the years long past.
7 At night I mused within my heart.
   I pondered and my spirit questioned.

8 " Will the Lord reject us for ever?
   Will he show us his favour no more?
9 Has his love vanished for ever?
   Has his promise come to an end?
10 Does God forget his mercy
   or in anger withhold his compassion?"

11 I said : " This is what causes my grief;
   that the way of the Most High has changed."
12 I remember the deeds of the Lord,
   I remember your wonders of old,
13 I muse on all your works
   and ponder your mighty deeds.

14 Your ways, O God, are holy.
   What god is great as our God?
15 You are the God who works wonders.
   You showed your power among the peoples.
16 Your strong arm redeemed your people,
   the sons of Jacob and Joseph.

17 The waters saw you, O God,
the waters saw you and trembled;
the depths were moved with terror.
18 The clouds poured down rain,
the skies sent forth their voice;
your arrows flashed to and fro.

19 Your thunder rolled round the sky,
your flashes lighted up the world.
The earth was moved and trembled
20 when your way led through the sea,
your path through the mighty waters
and no one saw your footprints.

21 You guided your people like a flock
by the hand of Moses and Aaron.

77

God's patience and man's ingratitude:
the lesson of past history

1 Give heed, my people to my teaching;
   turn your ear to the words of my mouth.
2 I will open my mouth in a parable
   and reveal hidden lessons of the past.

3 The things we have heard and understood,
   the things our fathers have told us
4 we will not hide from their children
   but will tell them to the next generation:

   the glories of the Lord and his might
   and the marvellous deeds he has done,
5 the witness he gave to Jacob,
   the law he established in Israel.

   He gave a command to our fathers
   to make it known to their children
6 that the next generation might know it,
   the children yet to be born.

7 They too should arise and tell their sons
   that they too should set their hope in God
   and never forget God's deeds
   but keep every one of his commands:

8 so that they might not be like their fathers,
   a defiant and rebellious race,
   a race whose heart was fickle,
   whose spirit was unfaithful to God.

*   *   *

9 The sons of Ephraim, armed with the bow,
   turned back in the day of battle.
10 They failed to keep God's covenant
   and would not walk according to his law.

11 They forgot the things he had done,
   the marvellous deeds he had shown them.
12 He did wonders in the sight of their fathers,
   in Egypt, in the plains of Zoan.

13 He divided the sea and led them through
   and made the waters stand up like a wall.
14 By day he led them with a cloud:
   by night, with a light of fire.

15 He split the rocks in the desert.
   He gave them plentiful drink as from the deep.
16 He made streams flow out from the rock
   and made waters run down like rivers.

*   *   *

17 Yet still they sinned against him;
   they defied the Most High in the desert.
18 In their heart they put God to the test
   by demanding the food they craved.

19 They even spoke against God.
   They said: "Is it possible for God
   to prepare a table in the desert?

20 It was he who struck the rock,
   water flowed and swept down in torrents.
   But can he also give us bread?
   Can he provide meat for his people?"

21 When he heard this the Lord was angry.
   A fire was kindled against Jacob,
   his anger rose against Israel
22 for having no faith in God;
   for refusing to trust in his help.

23 Yet he commanded the clouds above
   and opened the gates of heaven.
24 He rained down manna for their food,
   and gave them bread from heaven.

25 Mere men ate the bread of angels.
   He sent them abundance of food:
26 he made the east wind blow from heaven
   and roused the south wind by his might.

27 He rained food on them like dust,
   winged fowl like the sands of the sea.
28 He let it fall in the midst of their camp
   and all around their tents.

29 So they ate and had their fill;
   for he gave them all they craved.
30 But before they had sated their craving,
   while the food was still in their mouths,

31 God's anger rose against them.
   He slew the strongest among them,
   struck down the flower of Israel.

32 Despite this they went on sinning;
   they had no faith in his wonders:
33 so he ended their days like a breath
   and their years in sudden ruin.

34 When he slew them then they would seek him,
   return and seek him in earnest.
35 They would remember that God was their rock,
   God the Most High their redeemer.

36 But the words they spoke were mere flattery;
   they lied to him with their lips.
37 For their hearts were not truly with him;
   they were not faithful to his covenant.

38 Yet he who is full of compassion
   forgave their sin and spared them.
   So often he held back his anger
   when he might have stirred up his rage.

39 He remembered they were only men,
   a breath that passes never to return.

*   *   *

40 How often they defied him in the wilderness
and caused him pain in the desert!

41 Yet again they put God to the test
and grieved the Holy One of Israel.
42 They did not remember his deeds
nor the day he saved them from the foe;

43 when he worked his miracles in Egypt,
his wonders in the plains of Zoan:
44 when he turned their rivers into blood
and made their streams impossible to drink.

45 He sent dog-flies against them to devour them
and swarms of frogs to molest them.
46 He gave their crops to the grub,
the fruit of their labour to the locust.

47 He destroyed their vines with hail,
their sycamore trees with frost.
48 He gave up their cattle to plague,
their flocks and herds to pestilence.

49 He turned on them the heat of his anger,
fury, rage and havoc,
a troop of destroying angels.
50 He gave free course to his anger.

He did not spare them from death
but gave their lives to the plague.
51 He struck all the first-born in Egypt,
the finest flower in the dwellings of Ham.

52 Then he brought forth his people like sheep;
like a flock he guided them in the desert.
53 He led them safely with nothing to fear,
while the sea engulfed their foes.

54 So he brought them to his holy land,
to the mountain which his right hand had won.
55 He drove out the nations before them,
and divided the land for their heritage.

Their tents he gave as a dwelling
to each one of Israel's tribes.

*   *   *

56 Still they put God to the proof and defied him;
   they refused to obey the Most High.

57 They strayed, as faithless as their fathers,
   like a bow on which the archer cannot count.
58 They angered him with their mountain shrines;
   made him jealous with the idols they served.

59 God saw this and was filled with fury:
   he utterly rejected Israel.
60 He forsook his dwelling place in Shiloh,
   the tent where he lived among men.

61 He gave his ark into captivity,
   his glorious ark into the hands of the foe.
62 He gave up his people to the sword,
   in his anger against his chosen ones.

63 So war devoured their young men,
   their maidens had no wedding songs;
64 their priests fell by the sword
   and their widows made no lament.

65 Then the Lord awoke as if from sleep,
   like a warrior overcome with wine.
66 He struck his enemies from behind
   and put them to everlasting shame.

67 He rejected the tent of Joseph;
   He did not choose the tribe of Ephraim
68 but he chose the tribe of Judah,
   the hill of Sion which he loves.

69 He built his shrine like the heavens,
   or like the earth which he made firm for ever.
70 And he chose David his servant
   and took him away from the sheepfolds.

71 From the care of the ewes he called him
   to be shepherd of Jacob his people,
   of Israel his own possession.
72 He tended them with blameless heart,
   with discerning mind he led them.

78

National lament over the destruction of Jerusalem

1 O God, the nations have invaded your land,
   they have profaned your holy temple.
   They have made Jerusalem a heap of ruins.
2 They have handed over the bodies of your servants
   as food to feed the birds of heaven
   and the flesh of your faithful to the beasts of the earth.

3 They have poured out blood like water in Jerusalem,
   leaving no one to bury the dead.
4 We have become the taunt of our neighbours,
   the mockery and scorn of those who surround us.
5 How long, O Lord? Will you be angry for ever,
   how long will your anger burn like fire?

6 Pour out your rage on the nations,
   the nations that do not know you.
   Pour out your rage on the kingdoms
   that do not call on your name;
7 for they have devoured Jacob
   and laid waste the land where he dwells.

8 Do not hold the guilt of our fathers against us.
   Let your compassion hasten to meet us
   for we are in the depths of distress.
9 O God our saviour, come to our help,
   come for the sake of the glory of your name.
   O Lord our God, forgive us our sins;
   rescue us for the sake of your name.

10 Why should the nations say: "Where is their God?"
   Let us see the nations around us repaid
   with vengeance for the blood of your servants that was
       shed!
11 Let the groans of the prisoners come before you;
   let your strong arm reprieve those condemned to die

12 Pay back to our neighbours seven times over
   the taunts with which they taunted you, O Lord
13 But we, your people, the flock of your pasture,
   will give you thanks for ever and ever.
   We will tell your praise from age to age.

79

Plea for the return of God's favour

2 O shepherd of Israel, hear us,
  you who lead Joseph's flock,
  shine forth from your cherubim throne
3 upon Ephraim, Benjamin, Manasseh.
  O Lord, rouse up your might,
  O Lord, come to our help.

4 God of hosts, bring us back;
  let your face shine on us and we shall be saved.

5 Lord God of hosts, how long
  will you frown on your people's plea?
6 You have fed them with tears for their bread,
  an abundance of tears for their drink.
7 You have made us the taunt of our neighbours,
  our enemies laugh us to scorn.

8 God of hosts, bring us back;
  let your face shine on us and we shall be saved.

9 You brought a vine out of Egypt;
  to plant it you drove out the nations.
10 Before it you cleared the ground;
  it took root and spread through the land.

11 The mountains were covered with its shadow,
  the cedars of God with its boughs.
12 It stretched out its branches to the sea,
  to the Great River it stretched out its shoots.

13 Then why have you broken down its walls?
  It is plucked by all who pass by.
14 It is ravaged by the boar of the forest,
  devoured by the beasts of the field.

15 God of hosts, turn again, we implore,
   look down from heaven and see.
   Visit this vine 16 and protect it,
   the vine your right hand has planted.
17 Men have burnt it with fire and destroyed it.
   May they perish at the frown of your face.

18 May your hand be on the man you have chosen
   the man you have given your strength.
19 And we shall never forsake you again:
   give us life that we may call upon your name.

20 God of hosts, bring us back;
   let your face shine on us and we shall be saved

80

Festal song in harvest time

2 Ring out your joy to God our strength,
  shout in triumph to the God of Jacob.

3 Raise a song and sound the timbrel,
  the sweet-sounding harp and the lute,
4 blow the trumpet at the new moon,
  when the moon is full, on our feast.

5 For this is Israel's law,
  a command of the God of Jacob.
6 He imposed it as a rule on Joseph,
  when he went out against the land of Egypt.

  A voice I did not know said to me:
7 "I freed your shoulder from the burden;
  your hands were freed from the load.
8 You called in distress and I saved you.

  I answered, concealed in the storm cloud
  at the waters of Meribah I tested you.
9 Listen, my people, to my warning,
  O Israel, if only you would heed!

10 Let there be no foreign god among you,
  no worship of an alien god.
11 I am the Lord your God,
  who brought you from the land of Egypt.
  Open wide your mouth and I will fill it.

12 But my people did not heed my voice
  and Israel would not obey,
13 so I left them in their stubbornness of heart
  to follow their own designs.

14 O that my people would heed me,
  that Israel would walk in my ways!
15 At once I would subdue their foes,
  turn my hand against their enemies.

16 The Lord's enemies would cringe at their feet
   and their subjection would last for ever.
   But Israel I would feed with finest wheat
   and fill them with honey from the rock."

81

Judgment on corrupt authority

1 God stands in the divine assembly.
  In the midst of the gods he gives judgment.

2 "How long will you judge unjustly
  and favour the cause of the wicked?
3 Do justice for the weak and the orphan,
  defend the afflicted and the needy.
4 Rescue the weak and the poor;
  set them free from the hand of the wicked.

5 Unperceiving, they grope in the darkness
  and the order of the world is shaken.
6 I have said to you : 'You are gods
  and all of you, sons of the Most High.'
7 And yet, you shall die like men,
  you shall fall like any of the princes."

8 Arise, O God, judge the earth,
  for you rule all the nations.

82

A nation's appeal to God
for help against destruction

2 O God, do not keep silent,
  do not be dumb and unmoved, O God,
3 for your enemies raise a tumult.
  Those who hate you lift up their heads.

4 They plot against your people,
  conspire against those you love.
5 They say: "Come, let us destroy them as a nation;
  let the name of Israel be forgotten."
6 They conspire with a single mind,
  they make common alliance against you,

7 the camps of Edom and of Ishmael,
  the camps of Moab and Hagar,
8 the land of Ammon and Amalek,
  Philistia, with the people of Tyre.
9 Assyria too is their ally
  and joins hands with the sons of Lot.

10 Treat them like Midian, like Sisera,
  like Jabin at the River Kishon,
11 the men who were destroyed at Endor,
  whose bodies rotted on the ground.

12 Make their captains like Oreb and Zeëb,
  all their princes like Zebah and Zalmunna,
13 the men who said: "Let us take
  the fields of God for ourselves."
14 My God, scatter them like chaff,
  drive them like straw in the wind!

15 As fire that burns away the forest,
  as the flame that sets the mountains ablaze,
16 drive them away with your tempest
  and fill them with terror at your storm.

17 Cover their faces with shame,
   till they seek your name, O Lord.

18 Shame and terror be theirs for ever,
   let them be disgraced, let them perish!
19 Let them know that your name is the Lord,
   the Most High over all the earth.

83

Love and longing for God's temple

2 How lovely is your dwelling place,
Lord, God of hosts.

3 My soul is longing and yearning,
is yearning for the courts of the Lord.
My heart and my soul ring out their joy
to God, the living God.

4 The sparrow herself finds a home
and the swallow a nest for her brood;
she lays her young by your altars,
Lord of hosts, my king and my God.

5 They are happy, who dwell in your house,
for ever singing your praise.
6 They are happy, whose strength is in you,
in whose hearts are the roads to Sion.

7 As they go through the Bitter Valley
they make it a place of springs,
the autumn rain covers it with blessings.
8 They walk with ever growing strength,
they will see the God of gods in Sion.

9 O Lord God of hosts, hear my prayer,
give ear, O God of Jacob.
10 Turn your eyes, O God, our shield,
look on the face of your anointed.

11 One day within your courts
is better than a thousand elsewhere.
The threshold of the house of God
I prefer to the dwellings of the wicked.

12 For the Lord God is a rampart, a shield;
 he will give us his favour and glory.
 The Lord will not refuse any good
 to those who walk without blame.

13 Lord, God of hosts,
 happy the man who trusts in you!

84

The coming age of peace and justice

2 O Lord, you once favoured your land
and revived the fortunes of Jacob,
3 you forgave the guilt of your people
and covered all their sins.
4 You averted all your rage,
you calmed the heat of your anger.

5 Revive us now, God, our helper!
Put an end to your grievance against us.
6 Will you be angry with us for ever,
will your anger never cease?

7 Will you not restore again our life
that your people may rejoice in you?
8 Let us see, O Lord, your mercy
and give us your saving help.

* * *

9 I will hear what the Lord God has to say,
a voice that speaks of peace,
peace for his people and his friends
and those who turn to him in their hearts.
10 His help is near for those who fear him
and his glory will dwell in our land.

11 Mercy and faithfulness have met;
justice and peace have embraced.
12 Faithfulness shall spring from the earth
and justice look down from heaven.

13 The Lord will make us prosper
and our earth shall yield its fruit.
14 Justice shall march before him
and peace shall follow his steps.

85

Loyalty in God's service

1 Turn your ear, O Lord, and give answer
  for I am poor and needy.
2 Preserve my life, for I am faithful:
  save the servant who trusts in you.

3 You are my God, have mercy on me, Lord
  for I cry to you all the day long.
4 Give joy to your servant, O Lord,
  for to you I lift up my soul.

5 O Lord, you are good and forgiving,
  full of love to all who call.
6 Give heed, O Lord, to my prayer
  and attend to the sound of my voice.

7 In the day of distress I will call
  and surely you will reply.
8 Among the gods there is none like you, O Lord;
  nor work to compare with yours.

9 All the nations shall come to adore you
  and glorify your name, O Lord:
10 for you are great and do marvellous deeds,
  you who alone are God.

11 Show me, Lord, your way
  so that I may walk in your truth.
  Guide my heart to fear your name.

12 I will praise you, Lord my God, with all my heart
  and glorify your name for ever;
13 for your love to me has been great:
  you have saved me from the depths of the grave.

14 The proud have risen against me;
  ruthless men seek my life:
  to you they pay no heed.

15 But you, God of mercy and compassion,
slow to anger, O Lord,
abounding in love and truth,
16 turn and take pity on me.

O give your strength to your servant
and save your handmaid's son.
17 Show me a sign of your favour
that my foes may see to their shame
that you console me and give me your help.

86

God's city, mother of all nations

1 On the holy mountain is his city
2 cherished by the Lord.
  The Lord prefers the gates of Sion
  to all Jacob's dwellings.
3 Of you are told glorious things,
  O city of God!

4 "Babylon and Egypt I will count
  among those who know me;
  Philistia, Tyre, Ethiopia,
  these will be her children
5 and Sion shall be called 'Mother'
  for all shall be her children."

  It is he, the Lord Most High,
  who gives each his place.
6 In his register of peoples he writes:
  "These are her children"
7 and while they dance they will sing:
  "In you all find their home."

87

Prayer in desolation

2 Lord my God, I call for help by day;
  I cry at night before you.
3 Let my prayer come into your presence.
  O turn your ear to my cry.

4 For my soul is filled with evils;
  my life is on the brink of the grave.
5 I am reckoned as one in the tomb:
  I have reached the end of my strength,

6 like one alone among the dead;
  like the slain lying in their graves;
  like those you remember no more,
  cut off, as they are, from your hand.

7 You have laid me in the depths of the tomb,
  in places that are dark, in the depths.
8 Your anger weighs down upon me:
  I am drowned beneath your waves.

9 You have taken away my friends
  and made me hateful in their sight.
  Imprisoned, I cannot escape;
10 my eyes are sunken with grief.

  I call to you, Lord, all the day long;
  to you I stretch out my hands.
11 Will you work your wonders for the dead?
  Will the shades stand and praise you?

12 Will your love be told in the grave
  or your faithfulness among the dead?
13 Will your wonders be known in the dark
  or your justice in the land of oblivion?

14 As for me, Lord, I call to you for help :
  in the morning my prayer comes before you.
15 Lord, why do you reject me?
  Why do you hide your face?

16 Wretched, close to death from my youth,
  I have borne your trials; I am numb.
17 Your fury has swept down upon me;
  your terrors have utterly destroyed me.

18 They surround me all the day like a flood,
  they assail me all together.
19 Friend and neighbour you have taken away :
  my one companion is darkness.

88

The magnificent promises of God

2 I will sing for ever of your love, O Lord;
   through all ages my mouth will proclaim your truth.
3 Of this I am sure, that your love lasts for ever,
   that your truth is firmly established as the heavens.

4 " I have made a covenant with my chosen one;
   I have sworn to David my servant :
5 I will establish your dynasty for ever
   and set up your throne through all ages."

6 The heavens proclaim your wonders, O Lord;
   the assembly of your holy ones proclaim your truth.
7 For who in the skies can compare with the Lord
   or who is like the Lord among the sons of God?

8 A God to be feared in the council of the holy ones,
   great and dreadful to all around him.
9 O Lord God of hosts, who is your equal?
   You are mighty, O Lord, and truth is your garment.

10 It is you who rule the sea in its pride;
   it is you who still the surging of its waves.
11 It is you who trod Rahab underfoot like a corpse,
   scattering your foes with your mighty arm.

12 The heavens are yours, the world is yours.
   It is you who founded the earth and all it holds;
13 it is you who created the North and the South.
   Tabor and Hermon shout with joy at your name.

14 Yours is a mighty arm, O Lord;
   your hand is strong, your right hand ready.
15 Justice and right are the pillars of your throne,
   love and truth walk in your presence.

16 Happy the people who acclaim such a king,
   who walk, O Lord, in the light of your face,
17 who find their joy every day in your name,
   who make your justice the source of their bliss.

18 For it is you, O Lord, who are the glory of their
   strength;
   it is by your favour that our might is exalted:
19 for our ruler is in the keeping of the Lord;
   our king in the keeping of the Holy One of Israel.

                    *   *   *

20 Of old you spoke in a vision.
   To your friends the prophets you said:
   "I have set the crown on a warrior,
   I have exalted one chosen from the people.

21 I have found David my servant
   and with my holy oil anointed him.
22 My hand shall always be with him
   and my arm shall make him strong.

23 The enemy shall never outwit him
   nor the evil man oppress him.
24 I will beat down his foes before him
   and smite those who hate him.

25 My truth and my love shall be with him;
   by my name his might shall be exalted.
26 I will stretch out his hand to the Sea
   and his right hand as far as the River.

27 He will say to me: 'You are my father,
   my God, the rock who saves me.'
28 And I will make him my first-born,
   the highest of the kings of the earth.

29 I will keep my love for him always;
   for him my covenant shall endure.
30 I will establish his dynasty for ever,
   make his throne as lasting as the heavens.

31 If his sons forsake my law
   and refuse to walk as I decree
32 and if ever they violate my statutes,
   refusing to keep my commands;

33 then I will punish their offences with the rod,
   then I will scourge them on account of their guilt.
34 But I will never take back my love:
   my truth will never fail.

35 I will never violate my covenant
    nor go back on the word I have spoken.
36 Once for all, I have sworn by my holiness.
   'I will never lie to David.

37 His dynasty shall last for ever.
    In my sight his throne is like the sun;
38 like the moon, it shall endure for ever,
    a faithful witness in the skies.'"

* * *

39 And yet you have spurned, rejected,
    you are angry with the one you have anointed.
40 You have broken your covenant with your servant
    and dishonoured his crown in the dust.

41 You have broken down all his walls
    and reduced his fortresses to ruins.
42 He is despoiled by all who pass by:
    he has become the taunt of his neighbours.

43 You have exalted the right hand of his foes;
    you have made all his enemies rejoice.
44 You have made his sword give way,
    you have not upheld him in battle.

45 You have brought his glory to an end;
    you have hurled his throne to the ground.
46 You have cut short the years of his youth;
    you have heaped disgrace upon him.

47 How long, O Lord? Will you hide yourself for ever?
    How long will your anger burn like a fire?
48 Remember, Lord, the shortness of my life
    and how frail you have made the sons of men.
49 What man can live and never see death?
    Who can save himself from the grasp of the grave?

50 Where are your mercies of the past, O Lord,
    which you have sworn in your faithfulness to David?
51 Remember, Lord, how your servant is taunted,
    how I have to bear all the insults of the peoples.
52 Thus your enemies taunt me, O Lord,
    mocking your anointed at every step.

* * *

53 Blessed be the Lord for ever. Amen, amen!

89

Pondering on the brevity of life

1 O Lord, you have been our refuge
  from one generation to the next.
2 Before the mountains were born
  or the earth or the world brought forth,
  you are God, without beginning or end.

3 You turn men back into dust
  and say: "Go back, sons of men."
4 To your eyes a thousand years
  are like yesterday, come and gone,
  no more than a watch in the night.

5 You sweep men away like a dream,
  like grass which springs up in the morning.
6 In the morning it springs up and flowers:
  by evening it withers and fades.

7 So we are destroyed in your anger
  struck with terror in your fury.
8 Our guilt lies open before you;
  our secrets in the light of your face.

9 All our days pass away in your anger.
  Our life is over like a sigh.
10 Our span is seventy years
  or eighty for those who are strong.

  And most of these are emptiness and pain.
  They pass swiftly and we are gone.
11 Who understands the power of your anger
  and fears the strength of your fury?

12 Make us know the shortness of our life
  that we may gain wisdom of heart.
13 Lord, relent! Is your anger for ever?
  Show pity to your servants.

14 In the morning, fill us with your love;
   we shall exult and rejoice all our days.
15 Give us joy to balance our affliction
   for the years when we knew misfortune.

16 Show forth your work to your servants;
   let your glory shine on their children.
17 Let the favour of the Lord be upon us:
   give success to the work of our hands.
   (give success to the work of our hands).

90

Under the wing of God's protection

1 He who dwells in the shelter of the Most High
   and abides in the shade of the Almighty
2 says to the Lord : " My refuge,
   my stronghold, my God in whom I trust !"

3 It is he who will free you from the snare
   of the fowler who seeks to destroy you;
4 he will conceal you with his pinions
   and under his wings you will find refuge.

5 You will not fear the terror of the night
   nor the arrow that flies by day,
6 nor the plague that prowls in the darkness
   nor the scourge that lays waste at noon.

7 A thousand may fall at your side,
   ten thousand fall āt your right,
   you, it will never approach;
4c his faithfulness is buckler and shield.

8 Your eyes have only to look
   to see how the wicked are repaid,
9 you who have said : " Lord, my refuge !"
   and have made the Most High your dwelling.

10 Upon you no evil shall fall,
   no plague approach where you dwell.
11 For you has he commanded his angels,
   to keep you in all your ways.

12 They shall bear you upon their hands
   lest you strike your foot against a stone.
13 On the lion and the viper you will tread
   and trample the young lion and the dragon.

14 His love he set on me, so I will rescue him;
   protect him for he knows my name.
15 When he calls I shall answer: " I am with you."
   I will save him in distress and give him glory.

16 With length of life I will content him;
   I shall let him see my saving power.

91

Song of a happy man

2 It is good to give thanks to the Lord
  to make music to your name, O Most High,
3 to proclaim your love in the morning
  and your truth in the watches of the night,
4 on the ten-stringed lyre and the lute,
  with the murmuring sound of the harp.

5 Your deeds, O Lord, have made me glad;
  for the work of your hands I shout with joy
6 O Lord, how great are your works!
  How deep are your designs!
7 The foolish man cannot know this
  and the fool cannot understand.

8 Though the wicked spring up like grass
  and all who do evil thrive:
  they are doomed to be eternally destroyed.
9 But you, Lord, are eternally on high.
10 See how your enemies perish;
  all doers of evil are scattered.

11 To me you give the wild-ox's strength;
  you anoint me with the purest oil.
12 My eyes looked in triumph on my foes;
  my ears heard gladly of their fall.
13 The just will flourish like the palm-tree
  and grow like a Lebanon cedar.

14 Planted in the house of the Lord
  they will flourish in the courts of our God,
15 still bearing fruit when they are old,
  still full of sap, still green,
16 to proclaim that the Lord is just.
  in him, my rock, there is no wrong.

92

Praise of God, king of the world

1 The Lord is king, with majesty enrobed;
   the Lord has robed himself with might,
   he has girded himself with power.

   The world you made firm, not to be moved;
2 your throne has stood firm from of old.
   From all eternity, O Lord, you are.

3 The waters have lifted up, O Lord,
   the waters have lifted up their voice,
   the waters have lifted up their thunder.

4 Greater than the roar of mighty waters,
   more glorious than the surgings of the sea,
   the Lord is glorious on high.

5 Truly your decrees are to be trusted.
   Holiness is fitting to your house,
   O Lord, until the end of time.

93

God, the judge and vindicator

1 O Lord, avenging God,
  avenging God, appear!
2 Judge of the earth, arise,
  give the proud what they deserve!

3 How long, O Lord, shall the wicked,
  how long shall the wicked triumph?
4 They bluster with arrogant speech;
  the evil-doers boast to each other.

5 They crush your people, Lord,
  they afflict the ones you have chosen.
6 They kill the widow and the stranger
  and murder the fatherless child.

7 And they say: "The Lord does not see;
  the God of Jacob pays no heed."
8 Mark this, most senseless of people;
  fools, when will you understand?

9 Can he who made the ear, not hear?
  Can he who formed the eye, not see?
10 Will he who trains nations, not punish?
  Will he who teaches men, not have knowledge?
11 (The Lord knows the thoughts of men.
  He knows they are no more than a breath.)

12 Happy the man whom you teach, O Lord,
  whom you train by means of your law:
13 to him you give peace in evil days
  while the pit is being dug for the wicked.

14 The Lord will not abandon his people
  nor forsake those who are his own:
15 for judgment shall again be just
  and all true hearts shall uphold it.

16 Who will stand up for me against the wicked?
   Who will defend me against those who do evil?
17 If the Lord were not to help me,
   I would soon go down into the silence.

18 When I think: "I have lost my foothold";
   your mercy, Lord, holds me up.
19 When cares increase in my heart
   your consolation calms my soul.

20 Can judges who do evil be your friends?
   They do injustice under cover of law;
21 they attack the life of the just
   and condemn innocent blood.

22 As for me, the Lord will be a stronghold;
   my God will be the rock where I take refuge.
23 He will repay them for their wickedness,
   destroy them for their evil deeds.
   The Lord, our God, will destroy them.

94

Call to praise and worship:
a processional hymn

1 Come, ring out our joy to the Lord;
   hail the rock who saves us.
2 Let us come before him, giving thanks,
   with songs let us hail the Lord.

3 A mighty God is the Lord,
   a great king above all gods.
4 In his hand are the depths of the earth;
   the heights of the mountains are his.
5 To him belongs the sea, for he made it
   and the dry land shaped by his hands.

6 Come in; let us bow and bend low;
   let us kneel before the God who made us
7 for he is our God and we
   the people who belong to his pasture,
   the flock that is led by his hand.

O that to-day you would listen to his voice!
8 "Harden not your hearts as at Meribah,
   as on that day at Massah in the desert
9 when your fathers put me to the test;
   when they tried me, though they saw my work.

10 For forty years I was wearied of these people
   and I said: 'Their hearts are astray,
   these people do not know my ways.'
11 Then I took an oath in my anger:
   'Never shall they enter my rest.'"

95

The universal reign of the true God

1 O sing a new song to the Lord,
   sing to the Lord all the earth.
2 O sing to the Lord, bless his name.

   Proclaim his help day by day,
3 tell among the nations his glory
   and his wonders among all the peoples.

4 The Lord is great and worthy of praise,
   to be feared above all gods;
5 the gods of the heathens are naught.

   It was the Lord who made the heavens,
6 his are majesty and state and power
   and splendour in his holy place.

7 Give the Lord, you families of peoples,
   give the Lord glory and power,
8 give the Lord the glory of his name.

   Bring an offering and enter his courts,
9 worship the Lord in his temple.
   O earth, tremble before him.

10 Proclaim to the nations: "God is king."
   The world he made firm in its place;
   he will judge the peoples in fairness.

11 Let the heavens rejoice and earth be glad.
   let the sea and all within it thunder praise,
12 let the land and all it bears rejoice,
   all the trees of the wood shout for joy

13 at the presence of the Lord for he comes,
   he comes to rule the earth.
   With justice he will rule the world,
   he will judge the peoples with his truth.

96

Earth rejoices in its king

1 The Lord is king, let earth rejoice,
  the many coastlands be glad.
2 Cloud and darkness are his raiment;
  his throne, justice and right.

3 A fire prepares his path;
  it burns up his foes on every side.
4 His lightnings light up the world,
  the earth trembles at the sight.

5 The mountains melt like wax
  before the Lord of all the earth.
6 The skies proclaim his justice;
  all peoples see his glory.

7 Let those who serve idols be ashamed,
  those who boast of their worthless gods.
  All you spirits, worship him.

8 Sion hears and is glad;
  the people of Judah rejoice
  because of your judgments O Lord.

9 For you indeed are the Lord
  most high above all the earth
  exalted far above all spirits.

10 The Lord loves those who hate evil:
   he guards the souls of his saints;
   he sets them free from the wicked.

11 Light shines forth for the just
   and joy for the upright of heart.
12 Rejoice, you just, in the Lord;
   give glory to his holy name.

97

Orchestra of praise to God, king of the world

1 Sing a new song to the Lord
for he has worked wonders.
His right hand and his holy arm
have brought salvation.

2 The Lord has made known his salvation;
has shown his justice to the nations.
3 He has remembered his truth and love
for the house of Israel.

All the ends of the earth have seen
the salvation of our God.
4 Shout to the Lord all the earth,
ring out your joy.

5 Sing psalms to the Lord with the harp
with the sound of music.
6 With trumpets and the sound of the horn
acclaim the King, the Lord.

*   *   *

7 Let the sea and all within it, thunder;
the world, and all its peoples.
8 Let the rivers clap their hands
and the hills ring out their joy

9 at the presence of the Lord : for he comes,
he comes to rule the earth.
He will rule the world with justice
and the peoples with fairness.

98

The power and holiness of God

1 The Lord is king; the peoples tremble.
  He is throned on the cherubim; earth quakes.
2 The Lord is great in Sion.

  He is supreme over all the peoples.
3 Let them praise his name, so terrible and great.
  He is holy, 4 full of power.

  You are a king who loves what is right;
  you have established equity, justice and right;
  you have established them in Jacob.

5 Exalt the Lord our God;
  bow down before Sion, his footstool.
  He the Lord is holy.

6 Among his priests were Aaron and Moses,
  among those who invoked his name was Samuel.
  They invoked the Lord and he answered.

7 To them he spoke in the pillar of cloud.
  They did his will; they kept the law,
  which he, the Lord, had given.

8 O Lord our God, you answered them.
  For them you were a God who forgives,
  yet you punished all their offences.

9 Exalt the Lord our God;
  bow down before his holy mountain
  for the Lord our God is holy.

99

Praise to God, creator and shepherd

1 Cry out with joy to the Lord, all the earth
2 Serve the Lord with gladness.
Come before him, singing for joy.

3 Know that he, the Lord, is God.
He made us, we belong to him,
we are his people, the sheep of his flock.

4 Go within his gates, giving thanks.
Enter his courts with songs of praise.
Give thanks to him and bless his name.

5 Indeed, how good is the Lord,
eternal his merciful love.
He is faithful from age to age.

100

A pattern for rulers

1 My song is of mercy and justice;
  I sing to you, O Lord.
2 I will walk in the way of perfection.
  O when, Lord, will you come?

  I will walk with blameless heart
  within my house;
3 I will not set before my eyes
  whatever is base.

  I will hate the ways of the crooked;
  they shall not be my friends.
4 The false-hearted must keep far away;
  the wicked I disown.

5 The man who slanders his neighbour in secret
  I will bring to silence.
  The man of proud looks and haughty heart
  I will never endure.

6 I look to the faithful in the land
  that they may dwell with me.
  He who walks in the way of perfection
  shall be my friend.

7 No man who practises deceit
  shall live within my house.
  No man who utters lies shall stand
  before my eyes.

8 Morning by morning I will silence
  all the wicked in the land,
  uprooting from the Lord's city
  all who do evil.

101

Prayer for renewal:
fifth psalm of repentance

2 O Lord, listen to my prayer
and let my cry for help reach you.
3 Do not hide your face from me
in the day of my distress.
Turn your ear towards me
and answer me quickly when I call.

4 For my days are vanishing like smoke,
my bones burn away like a fire.
5 My heart is withered like the grass.
I forget to eat my bread.
6 I cry with all my strength
and my skin clings to my bones.

7 I have become like a pelican in the wilderness,
like an owl in desolate places.
8 I lie awake and I moan
like some lonely bird on a roof.
9 All day long my foes revile me;
those who hate me use my name as a curse.

10 The bread I eat is ashes;
my drink is mingled with tears.
11 In your anger, Lord, and your fury
you have lifted me up and thrown me down.
12 My days are like a passing shadow
and I wither away like the grass.

* * *

13 But you, O Lord, will endure for ever
and your name from age to age.
14 You will arise and have mercy on Sion:
for this is the time to have mercy,
(yes, the time appointed has come)
15 for your servants love her very stones,
are moved with pity even for her dust.

16 The nations shall fear the name of the Lord
   and all the earth's kings your glory,
17 when the Lord shall build up Sion again
   and appear in all his glory.
18 Then he will turn to the prayers of the helpless:
   he will not despise their prayers.

19 Let this be written for ages to come
   that a people yet unborn may praise the Lord;
20 for the Lord leaned down from his sanctuary on high.
   He looked down from heaven to the earth
21 that he might hear the groans of the prisoners
   and free those condemned to die.

29 The sons of your servants shall dwell untroubled
   and their race shall endure before you
22 that the name of the Lord may be proclaimed in Sion
   and his praise in the heart of Jerusalem,
23 when peoples and kingdoms are gathered together
   to pay their homage to the Lord.

* * *

24 He has broken my strength in mid-course;
   he has shortened the days of my life.
25 I say to God: "Do not take me away
   before my days are complete,
   you, whose days last from age to age.

26 Long ago you founded the earth
   and the heavens are the work of your hands.
27 They will perish but you will remain.
   They will all wear out like a garment.
   You will change them like clothes that are changed.
28 But you neither change, nor have an end."

102

Praise of God's love

1 My soul, give thanks to the Lord,
  all my being, bless his holy name.
2 My soul, give thanks to the Lord
  and never forget all his blessings.

3 It is he who forgives all your guilt,
  who heals every one of your ills,
4 who redeems your life from the grave,
  who crowns you with love and compassion,
5 who fills your life with good things,
  renewing your youth like an eagle's.

6 The Lord does deeds of justice,
  gives judgment for all who are oppressed.
7 He made known his ways to Moses
  and his deeds to Israel's sons.

8 The Lord is compassion and love,
  slow to anger and rich in mercy.
9 His wrath will come to an end;
  he will not be angry for ever.
10 He does not treat us according to our sins
  nor repay us according to our faults.

11 For as the heavens are high above the earth
  so strong is his love for those who fear him.
12 As far as the east is from the west
  so far does he remove our sins.

13 As a father has compassion on his sons,
  the Lord has pity on those who fear him;
14 for he knows of what we are made,
  he remembers that we are dust.

15 As for man, his days are like grass;
  he flowers like the flower of the field;
16 the wind blows and he is gone
  and his place never sees him again.

17 But the love of the Lord is everlasting
   upon those who hold him in fear;
   his justice reaches out to children's children
18 when they keep his covenant in truth,
   when they keep his will in their mind.

19 The Lord has set his sway in heaven
   and his kingdom is ruling over all.
20 Give thanks to the Lord, all his angels,
   mighty in power, fulfilling his word,
   who heed the voice of his word.

21 Give thanks to the Lord, all his hosts,
   his servants who do his will.
22 Give thanks to the Lord, all his works,
   in every place where he rules.
   My soul, give thanks to the Lord!

103

God's boundless care for his creation:
a psalm of worship

1 Bless the Lord, my soul!
  Lord God, how great you are,
  clothed in majesty and glory,
2 wrapped in light as in a robe!

*   *   *

You stretch out the heavens like a tent.
3 Above the rains you build your dwelling.
  You make the clouds your chariot,
  you walk on the wings of the wind,
4 you make the winds your messengers
  and flashing fire your servants.

5 You founded the earth on its base,
  to stand firm from age to age.
6 You wrapped it with the ocean like a cloak:
  the waters stood higher than the mountains.

7 At your threat they took to flight;
  at the voice of your thunder they fled.
8 They rose over the mountains and flowed down
  to the place which you had appointed.
9 You set limits they might not pass
  lest they return to cover the earth.

10 You make springs gush forth in the valleys:
   they flow in between the hills.
11 They give drink to all the beasts of the field;
   the wild-asses quench their thirst.
12 On their banks dwell the birds of heaven;
   from the branches they sing their song.

13 From your dwelling you water the hills;
   earth drinks its fill of your gift.
14 You make the grass grow for the cattle
   and the plants to serve man's needs,

that he may bring forth bread from the earth
15 and wine, to cheer man's heart;
oil, to make his face shine
and bread to strengthen man's heart.

16 The trees of the Lord drink their fill,
the cedars he planted on Lebanon;
17 there the birds build their nests:
on the tree-top the stork has her home.
18 The goats find a home on the mountains
and rabbits hide in the rocks.

19 You made the moon to mark the months;
the sun knows the time for its setting.
20 When you spread the darkness it is night
and all the beasts of the forest creep forth.
21 The young lions roar for their prey
and ask their food from God.

22 At the rising of the sun they steal away
and go to rest in their dens.
23 Man goes forth to his work,
to labour till evening falls.

24 How many are your works, O Lord!
In wisdom you have made them all.
The earth is full of your riches.

25 There is the sea, vast and wide,
with its moving swarms past counting,
living things great and small.
26 The ships are moving there
and the monsters you made to play with.

27 All of these look to you
to give them their food in due season.
28 You give it, they gather it up:
you open your hand, they have their fill.

29 You hide your face, they are dismayed;
you take back your spirit, they die,
returning to the dust from which they came.
30 You send forth your spirit, they are created;
and you renew the face of the earth.

31 May the glory of the Lord last for ever!
   May the Lord rejoice in his works!
32 He looks on the earth and it trembles;
   the mountains send forth smoke at his touch.

33 I will sing to the Lord all my life,
   make music to my God while I live.
34 May my thoughts be pleasing to him.
   I find my joy in the Lord.
35 Let sinners vanish from the earth
   and the wicked exist no more.

Bless the Lord, my soul.

104

God's faithfulness to his promise:
the story of Israel

Alleluia!

1 Give thanks to the Lord, tell his name,
  make known his deeds among the peoples.

2 O sing to him, sing his praise;
  tell all his wonderful works!
3 Be proud of his holy name,
  let the hearts that seek the Lord rejoice.

4 Consider the Lord and his strength;
  constantly seek his face.
5 Remember the wonders he has done,
  his miracles, the judgments he spoke.

6 O children of Abraham, his servant,
  O sons of the Jacob he chose.
7 He, the Lord, is our God:
  his judgments prevail in all the earth.

8 He remembers his covenant for ever,
  his promise for a thousand generations,
9 the covenant he made with Abraham,
  the oath he swore to Isaac.

10 He confirmed it for Jacob as a law,
   for Israel as a covenant for ever.
11 He said: "I am giving you a land,
   Canaan, your appointed heritage."

12 When they were few in number,
   a handful of strangers in the land,
13 when they wandered from country to country
   and from one kingdom to another,

14 he allowed no one to oppress them;
   he admonished kings on their account:
15 "Do not touch my anointed;
   do no harm to any of my prophets."

16 But he called down a famine on the land;
   he broke the staff that supported them.
17 He had sent a man before them,
   Joseph, sold as a slave.

18 His feet were put in chains,
   his neck was bound with iron,
19 until what he said came to pass
   and the Lord's word proved him true.

20 Then the king sent and released him;
   the ruler of the peoples set him free,
21 making him master of his house
   and ruler of all he possessed,

22 to instruct his princes as he pleased
   and to teach his elders wisdom.
23 So Israel came into Egypt,
   Jacob lived in the country of Ham.

24 He gave his people increase;
   he made them stronger than their foes,
25 whose hearts he turned to hate his people
   and to deal deceitfully with his servants.

26 Then he sent Moses his servant
   and Aaron the man he had chosen.
27 Through them he showed his marvels
   and his wonders in the country of Ham.

28 He sent darkness, and dark was made
   but Egypt resisted his words.
29 He turned the waters into blood
   and caused their fish to die.

30 Their land was alive with frogs,
   even in the halls of their kings.
31 He spoke; the dog-fly came
   and gnats covered the land.

32 He sent hail-stones in place of the rain
  and flashing fire in their land.
33 He struck their vines and fig-trees;
  he shattered the trees through their land.

34 He spoke; the locusts came,
  young locusts, too many to be counted.
35 They ate up every blade in the land;
  they ate up all the fruit of their fields.

36 He struck all the first-born in their land,
  the finest flower of their sons.
37 He led out Israel with silver and gold.
  In his tribes were none who fell behind.

38 Egypt rejoiced when they left
  for dread had fallen upon them.
39 He spread a cloud as a screen
  and fire to give light in the darkness.

40 When they asked for food he sent quails;
  he filled them with bread from heaven.
41 He pierced the rock to give them water;
  it gushed forth in the desert like a river.

42 For he remembered his holy word,
  which he gave to Abraham his servant.
43 So he brought out his people with joy,
  his chosen ones with shouts of rejoicing.

44 And he gave them the land of the nations.
  They took the fruit of other men's toil,
45 that thus they might keep his precepts,
  that thus they might observe his laws.

  Alleluia !

105

Ingratitude of man:
the story of Israel

1 Alleluia!

O give thanks to the Lord for he is good;
for his great love is without end.
2 Who can tell the Lord's mighty deeds?
Who can recount all his praise?

3 They are happy who do what is right,
who at all times do what is just.
4 O Lord, remember me
out of the love you have for your people.

Come to me, Lord, with your help
5 that I may see the joy of your chosen ones
and may rejoice in the gladness of your nation
and share the glory of your people.

6 Our sin is the sin of our fathers;
we have done wrong, our deeds have been evil.
7 Our fathers when they were in Egypt
paid no heed to your wonderful deeds.

They forgot the greatness of your love;
at the Red Sea defied the Most High.
8 Yet he saved them for the sake of his name,
in order to make known his power.

9 He threatened the Red Sea; it dried up
and he led them through the deep as through the
desert.
10 He saved them from the hand of the foe;
he saved them from the grip of the enemy.

11 The waters covered their oppressors;
not one of them was left alive.
12 Then they believed in his words:
then they sang his praises.

13 But they soon forgot his deeds
and would not wait upon his will.
14 They yielded to their cravings in the desert
and put God to the test in the wilderness.

15 He granted them the favour they asked
and sent disease among them.
16 Then they rebelled, envious of Moses
and of Aaron, the Lord's holy one.

17 The earth opened and swallowed up Dathan
and buried the clan of Abiram.
18 Fire blazed up against their clan
and flames devoured the rebels.

19 They fashioned a calf at Horeb
and worshipped an image of metal,
20 exchanging the God who was their glory
for the image of a bull that eats grass.

21 They forgot the God who was their saviour,
who had done such great things in Egypt,
22 such portents in the land of Ham,
such marvels at the Red Sea.

23 For this he said he would destroy them,
but Moses, the man he had chosen,
stood in the breach before him,
to turn back his anger from destruction.

24 Then they scorned the land of promise:
they had no faith in his word.
25 They complained inside their tents
and would not listen to the voice of the Lord.

26 So he raised his hand to swear an oath
that he would lay them low in the desert;
27 would scatter their sons among the nations
and disperse them throughout the lands.

28 They bowed before the Baal of Peor;
ate offerings made to lifeless gods.
29 They roused him to anger with their deeds
and a plague broke out among them.

30 Then Phinehas stood up and intervened.
   Thus the plague was ended
31 and this was counted in his favour
   from age to age for ever.

32 They provoked him at the waters of Meribah.
   Through their fault it went ill with Moses;
33 for they made his heart grow bitter
   and he uttered words that were rash.

34 They failed to destroy the peoples
   as the Lord had given command,
35 but instead they mingled with the nations
   and learned to act like them.

36 They worshipped the idols of the nations
   and these became a snare to entrap them.
37 They even offered their own sons
   and their daughters in sacrifice to demons.

38 They shed the blood of the innocent,
   the blood of their sons and daughters
   whom they offered to the idols of Canaan.
   The land was polluted with blood.

39 So they defiled themselves by their deeds
   and broke their marriage bond with the Lord
40 till his anger blazed against his people :
   he was filled with horror at his chosen ones.

41 So he gave them into the hand of the nations
   and their foes became their rulers.
42 Their enemies became their oppressors;
   they were subdued beneath their hand.

43 Time after time he rescued them,
   but in their malice they dared to defy him
   and sank low through their guilt.
44 In spite of this he paid heed to their distress,
   so often as he heard their cry.

45 For their sake he remembered his covenant.
   In the greatness of his love he relented
46 and he let them be treated with mercy
   by all who held them captive.

47 O Lord, our God, save us!
   Gather us from among the nations
   that we may thank your holy name
   and make it our glory to praise you.

*   *   *

48 Blessed be the Lord, God of Israel,
   for ever, from age to age.
   Let all the people cry out:
   "Amen! Amen! Alleluia!"

106

God's inexhaustible love

1 "O give thanks to the Lord for he is good;
  for his great love is without end."

2 Let them say this, the Lord's redeemed,
  whom he redeemed from the hand of the foe
3 and gathered from far-off lands,
  from east and west, north and south.

* * *

4 Some wandered in the desert, in the wilderness,
  finding no way to a city they could dwell in.
5 Hungry they were and thirsty;
  their soul was fainting within them.

6 Then they cried to the Lord in their need
  and he rescued them from their distress
7 and he led them along the right way,
  to reach a city they could dwell in.

8 Let them thank the Lord for his love,
  for the wonders he does for men.
9 For he satisfies the thirsty soul;
  he fills the hungry with good things,

* * *

10 Some lay in darkness and in gloom,
  prisoners in misery and chains,
11 having defied the words of God
  and spurned the counsels of the Most High.
12 He crushed their spirit with toil;
  they stumbled; there was no one to help.

13 Then they cried to the Lord in their need
  and he rescued them from their distress.
14 He led them forth from darkness and gloom
  and broke their chains to pieces.

15 Let them thank the Lord for his goodness,
   for the wonders he does for men:
16 for he bursts the gates of bronze
   and shatters the iron bars.

*　　*　　*

17 Some were sick on account of their sins
   and afflicted on account of their guilt.
18 They had a loathing for every food;
   they came close to the gates of death.

19 Then they cried to the Lord in their need
   and he rescued them from their distress.
20 He sent forth his word to heal them
   and saved their life from the grave.

21 Let them thank the Lord for his love,
   for the wonders he does for men.
22 Let them offer a sacrifice of thanks
   and tell of his deeds with rejoicing.

*　　*　　*

23 Some sailed to the sea in ships
   to trade on the mighty waters.
24 These men have seen the Lord's deeds,
   the wonders he does in the deep.

25 For he spoke; he summoned the gale,
   tossing the waves of the sea
26 up to heaven and back into the deep;
   their soul melted away in their distress.

27 They staggered, reeled like drunken men,
   for all their skill was gone.
28 Then they cried to the Lord in their need
   and he rescued them from their distress.

29 He stilled the storm to a whisper:
   all the waves of the sea were hushed.
30 They rejoiced because of the calm
   and he led them to the haven they desired.

31 Let them thank the Lord for his love,
   the wonders he does for men.
32 Let them exalt him in the gathering of the people
   and praise him in the meeting of the elders.

*   *   *

33 He changes streams into a desert,
   springs of water into thirsty ground,
34 a fruitful land into a salt waste,
   for the wickedness of those who live there.

35 But he changes desert into streams,
   thirsty ground into springs of water.
36 There he settles the hungry
   and they built a city to dwell in.

37 They sow fields and plant their vines;
   these yield crops for the harvest.
38 He blesses them; they grow in numbers.
   He does not let their herds decrease.

*   *   *

40 He pours contempt upon princes,
   makes them wander in trackless wastes.
39 They diminish, are reduced to nothing
   by oppression, evil and sorrow.

41 But he raises the needy from distress;
   makes families numerous as a flock.
42 The upright see it and rejoice
   but all who do wrong are silenced.

43 Whoever is wise, let him heed these things
   and consider the love of the Lord.

107

Prayer for victory

2 My heart is ready, O God;
  I will sing, sing your praise.
  Awake, my soul;
3 awake, lyre and harp.
  I will awake the dawn.

4 I will thank you, Lord, among the peoples,
  praise you among the nations;
5 for your love reaches to the heavens
  and your truth to the skies.
6 O God, arise above the heavens;
  may your glory shine on earth!

7 O come and deliver your friends;
  help with your right hand and reply.
8 From his holy place God has made this promise:
  "I will triumph and divide the land of Shechem;
  I will measure out the valley of Succoth.

9 Gilead is mine and Manasseh.
  Ephraim I take for my helmet,
  Judah for my commander's staff.
10 Moab I will use for my washbowl,
  on Edom I will plant my shoe.
  Over the Philistines I will shout in triumph."

11 But who will lead me to conquer the fortress?
  Who will bring me face to face with Edom?
12 Will you utterly reject us, O God,
  and no longer march with our armies?

13 Give us help against the foe:
  for the help of man is vain.
14 With God we shall do bravely
  and he will trample down our foes.

108

Appeal for help against vicious enemies

1 O God whom I praise, do not be silent:
2 for the mouths of deceit and wickedness
are opened against me.

3 They speak to me with lying tongues;
they beset me with words of hate
and attack me without cause.

4 In return for my love they accuse me
while I pray for them.
5 They repay me evil for good,
hatred for love.

*   *   *

6 Appoint a wicked man as his judge:
let an accuser stand at his right.
7 When he is judged let him come out condemned;
let his prayer be considered as sin.

8 Let the days of his life be few;
let another man take his office.
9 Let his children become fatherless orphans
and his wife become a widow.

10 Let his children be wanderers and beggars
driven from the ruins of their home.
11 let the creditor seize all his goods;
let strangers take the fruit of his work.

12 Let none show him any mercy
nor pity his fatherless children.
13 Let all his sons be destroyed
and with them their name be blotted out.

14 Let his father's guilt be remembered,
his mother's sin be retained.
15 Let it always stand before the Lord,
that their memory may be cut off from the earth.

16 For he did not think of showing mercy
   but pursued the poor and the needy,
   hounding the wretched to death.
17 He loved cursing; let curses fall on him.
   He scorned blessing; let blessing pass him by.

18 He put on cursing like his coat;
   let it soak into his body like water;
   let it sink like oil into his bones;
19 let it be like the clothes that cover him,
   like a girdle he cannot take off!

*   *   *

20 Let the Lord thus repay my accusers,
   all those who speak evil against me.
21 For your name's sake act in my defence;
   in the goodness of your love be my rescuer.

22 For I am poor and needy
   and my heart is pierced within me.
23 I fade like an evening shadow;
   I am shaken off like a locust.

24 My knees are weak from fasting;
   my body is thin and gaunt.
25 I have become an object of scorn,
   all who see me toss their heads.

26 Help me, Lord my God;
   save me because of your love.
27 Let them know that this is your work,
   that this is your doing, O Lord.

28 They may curse but you will bless.
   Let my attackers be put to shame
   but let your servant rejoice.
29 Let my accusers be clothed with dishonour,
   covered with shame as with a cloak.

30 Loud thanks to the Lord are on my lips.
   I will praise him in the midst of the throng,
31 for he stands at the poor man's side
   to save him from those who condemn him.

109

The Messiah, king, priest and judge

1 The Lord's revelation to my Master:
" Sit on my right:
I will put your foes beneath your feet."

2 The Lord will send from Sion
your sceptre of power:
rule in the midst of all your foes.

3 A prince from the day of your birth
on the holy mountains;
from the womb before the daybreak I begot you.

5 The Lord has sworn an oath he will not change.
" You are a priest for ever,
a priest like Melchizedeck of old."

*   *   *

5 The Master standing at your right hand
will shatter kings in the day of his great wrath

6 He, the Judge of the nations,
will heap high the bodies;
heads shall be shattered far and wide.

He shall drink from the stream by the wayside
and therefore he shall lift up his head.

110

The great works of God:
an alphabetical psalm

1 Alleluia!

  I will thank the Lord with all my heart
  in the meeting of the just and their assembly.
2 Great are the works of the Lord;
  to be pondered by all who love them.

3 Majestic and glorious his work,
  his justice stands firm for ever.
4 He makes us remember his wonders.
  The Lord is compassion and love.

5 He gives food to those who fear him;
  keeps his covenant ever in mind.
6 He has shown his might to his people
  by giving them the lands of the nations.

7 His works are justice and truth:
  his precepts are all of them sure,
8 standing firm for ever and ever:
  they are made in uprightness and truth.

9 He has sent deliverance to his people
  and established his covenant for ever.
  Holy his name, to be feared.

10 To fear the Lord is the beginning of wisdom;
  all who do so prove themselves wise.
  His praise shall last for ever!

I I I

The generous and upright man:
an alphabetical psalm

1 Alleluia!

   Happy the man who fears the Lord,
   who takes delight in his commands.
2 His sons will be powerful on earth;
   the children of the upright are blessed.

3 Riches and wealth are in his house;
   his justice stands firm for ever.
4 He is a light in the darkness for the upright:
   he is generous, merciful and just.

5 The good man takes pity and lends,
   he conducts his affairs with honour.
6 The just man will never waver:
   he will be remembered for ever.

7 He has no fear of evil news;
   with a firm heart he trusts in the Lord.
8 With a steadfast heart he will not fear;
   he will see the downfall of his foes.

9 Open-handed, he gives to the poor;
   his justice stands firm for ever.
   His head will be raised in glory.

10 The wicked man sees and is angry,
   gnashes his teeth and pines away;
   the desire of the wicked leads to doom.

112

To the God of glory and compassion:
a psalm of worship

1 Alleluia!

Praise, O servants of the Lord,
praise the name of the Lord!
2 May the name of the Lord be blessed
both now and for evermore!
3 From the rising of the sun to its setting
praised be the name of the Lord!

4 High above all nations is the Lord,
above the heavens his glory.
5 Who is like the Lord, our God,
who has risen on high to his throne
6 yet stoops from the heights to look down,
to look down upon heaven and earth?

7 From the dust he lifts up the lowly,
from the dungheap he raises the poor
8 to set him in the company of princes,
yes, with the princes of his people.
9 To the childless wife he gives a home
and gladdens her heart with children.

113

The wonders of the Exodus: the one true God

1 Alleluia!

  When Israel came forth from Egypt,
  Jacob's sons from an alien people,
2 Judah became the Lord's temple,
  Israel became his kingdom.

3 The sea fled at the sight:
  the Jordan turned back on its course,
4 the mountains leapt like rams
  and the hills like yearling sheep.

5 Why was it, sea, that you fled,
  that you turned back, Jordan, on your course?
6 Mountains, that you leapt like rams,
  hills, like yearling sheep?

7 Tremble, O earth, before the Lord,
  in the presence of the God of Jacob,
8 who turns the rock into a pool
  and flint into a spring of water.

(Psalm 115 in the Hebrew text)

1 Not to us, Lord, not to us,
  but to your name give the glory
  for the sake of your love and your truth,
2 lest the heathen say: "Where is their God?"

3 But our God he is in the heavens;
  he does whatever he wills.
4 Their idols are silver and gold,
  the work of human hands.

5 They have mouths but they cannot speak;
  they have eyes but they cannot see;
6 they have ears but they cannot hear;
  they have nostrils but they cannot smell.

7 With their hands they cannot feel;
   with their feet they cannot walk.
   No sound comes from their throats.
8 Their makers will become like them:
   so will all who trust in them.

9 Sons of Israel, trust in the Lord;
   he is their help and their shield.
10 Sons of Aaron, trust in the Lord;
   he is their help and their shield.

11 You who fear him, trust in the Lord;
   he is their help and their shield.
12 He remembers us, will give us his blessing;
   he will bless the sons of Israel.
   He will bless the sons of Aaron.

13 The Lord will bless those who fear him,
   the little no less than the great:
14 to you may the Lord grant increase,
   to you and all your children.

15 May you be blessed by the Lord,
   the maker of heaven and earth.
16 The heavens belong to the Lord
   but the earth he has given to men.

17 The dead shall not praise the Lord,
   nor those who go down into the silence.
18 But we who live bless the Lord
   now and for ever. Amen.

114

Prayer of a man saved from death

1 Alleluia!

   I love the Lord for he has heard
      the cry of my appeal;
2 for he turned his ear to me
      in the day when I called him.

3 They surrounded me, the snares of death,
      with the anguish of the tomb;
   they caught me, sorrow and distress.
4 I called on the Lord's name.

   O Lord my God, deliver me!

5 How gracious is the Lord, and just;
      our God has compassion.
6 The Lord protects the simple hearts;
      I was helpless so he saved me.

7 Turn back, my soul, to your rest
      for the Lord has been good;
8 he has kept my soul from death,
      (my eyes from tears)
      and my feet from stumbling.

9 I will walk in the presence of the Lord
      in the land of the living.

115

Promise in gratitude to God

10 I trusted, even when I said:
  " I am sorely afflicted,"
11 and when I said in my alarm:
  " No man can be trusted."

12 How can I repay the Lord
  for his goodness to me?
13 The cup of salvation I will raise;
  I will call on the Lord's name.

14 My vows to the Lord I will fulfil
  before all his people.
15 O precious in the eyes of the Lord
  is the death of his faithful.

16 Your servant, Lord, your servant am I;
  you have loosened my bonds.
17 A thanksgiving sacrifice I make:
  I will call on the Lord's name.

18 My vows to the Lord I will fulfil
  before all his people,
19 in the courts of the house of the Lord,
  in your midst, O Jerusalem.

116

World-wide call to praise God

1 Alleluia!

O praise the Lord, all you nations,
acclaim him all you peoples!

2 Strong is his love for us;
he is faithful for ever.

117

Processional song of praise

1 Alleluia!

Give thanks to the Lord for he is good,
for his love has no end.

       *　 *　 *

2 Let the sons of Israel say:
"His love has no end."
3 Let the sons of Aaron say:
"His love has no end."
4 Let those who fear the Lord say:
"His love has no end."

5 I called to the Lord in my distress;
he answered and freed me.
6 The Lord is at my side; I do not fear.
What can man do against me?
7 The Lord is at my side as my helper:
I shall look down on my foes.

8 It is better to take refuge in the Lord
than to trust in men:
9 it is better to take refuge in the Lord
than to trust in princes.

10 The nations all encompassed me;
in the Lord's name I crushed them.
11 They compassed me, compassed me about;
in the Lord's name I crushed them.
12 They compassed me about like bees;
they blazed like a fire among thorns.
In the Lord's name I crushed them.

13 I was thrust, thrust down and falling
but the Lord was my helper.
14 The Lord is my strength and my song;
he was my saviour.
15 There are shouts of joy and victory
in the tents of the just.

The Lord's right hand has triumphed;
16 his right hand raised me up.
The Lord's right hand has triumphed;
17 I shall not die, I shall live
and recount his deeds.
18 I was punished, I was punished by the Lord
but not doomed to die.

19 Open to me the gates of holiness:
I will enter and give thanks.
20 This is the Lord's own gate
where the just may enter.
21 I will thank you for you have given answer
and you are my saviour.

22 The stone which the builders rejected
has become the corner stone.
23 This is the work of the Lord,
a marvel in our eyes.
24 This day was made by the Lord;
we rejoice and are glad.

25 O Lord, grant us salvation;
O Lord, grant success.
26 Blessed in the name of the Lord
is he who comes.
We bless you from the house of the Lord;
27 the Lord God is our light.

Go forward in procession with branches
even to the altar.
28 You are my God, I thank you.
My God, I praise you
29 Give thanks to the Lord for he is good;
for his love has no end.

118

Love of God's law:
an alphabetical psalm

ALEPH

1 They are happy whose life is blameless,
  who follow God's law!
2 They are happy those who do his will,
  seeking him with all their hearts,
3 who never do anything evil
  but walk in his ways.
4 You have laid down your precepts
  to be obeyed with care.
5 May my footsteps be firm
  to obey your statutes.
6 Then I shall not be put to shame
  as I heed your commands.
7 I will thank you with an upright heart
  as I learn your decrees.
8 I will obey your statutes:
  do not forsake me.

BETH

9 How shall the young remain sinless?
  By obeying your word.
10 I have sought you with all my heart:
  let me not stray from your commands.
11 I treasure your promise in my heart
  lest I sin against you.
12 Blessed are you, O Lord;
  teach me your statutes.
13 With my tongue I have recounted
  the decrees of your lips.
14 I rejoiced to do your will
  as though all riches were mine.
15 I will ponder all your precepts
  and consider your paths.

16 I take delight in your statutes;
   I will not forget your word.

GIMEL

17 Bless your servant and I shall live
   and obey your word.
18 Open my eyes that I may consider
   the wonders of your law.
19 I am a pilgrim on the earth;
   show me your commands.
20 My soul is ever consumed
   in longing for your decrees.
21 You threaten the proud, the accursed,
   who turn from your commands.
22 Relieve me from scorn and contempt
   for I do your will.
23 Though princes sit plotting against me
   I ponder on your statutes.
24 Your will is my delight;
   your statutes are my counsellors.

DALETH

25 My soul lies in the dust;
   by your word revive me.
26 I declared my ways and you answered:
   teach me your statutes.
27 Make me grasp the way of your precepts
   and I will muse on your wonders.
28 My soul pines away with grief;
   by your word raise me up.
29 Keep me from the way of error
   and teach me your law.
30 I have chosen the way of truth
   with your decrees before me.
31 I bind myself to do your will;
   Lord, do not disappoint me.
32 I will run the way of your commands;
   you give freedom to my heart.

HE

33 Teach me the demands of your statutes
   and I will keep them to the end.

34 Train me to observe your law,
  to keep it with my heart.
35 Guide me in the path of your commands;
  for there is my delight.
36 Bend my heart to your will
  and not to love of gain.
37 Keep my eyes from what is false:
  by your word, give me life.
38 Keep the promise you have made
  to the servant who fears you.
39 Keep me from the scorn I dread,
  for your decrees are good.
40 See, I long for your precepts:
  then in your justice, give me life.

VAU

41 Lord, let your love come upon me,
  the saving help of your promise.
42 And I shall answer those who taunt me
  for I trust in your word.
43 Do not take the word of truth from my mouth
  for I trust in your decrees.
44 I shall always keep your law
  for ever and ever.
45 I shall walk in the path of freedom
  for I seek your precepts.
46 I will speak of your will before kings
  and not be abashed.
47 Your commands have been my delight;
  these I have loved.
48 I will worship your commands and love them
  and ponder your statutes.

ZAYIN

49 Remember your word to your servant
  by which you gave me hope.
50 This is my comfort in sorrow
  that your promise gives me life.
51 Though the proud may utterly deride me
  I keep to your law.
52 I remember your decrees of old
  and these, Lord, console me.

53 I am seized with indignation at the wicked
   who forsake your law.
54 Your statutes have become my song
   in the land of exile.
55 I think of your name in the night-time
   and I keep your law.
56 This has been my blessing,
   the keeping of your precepts.

HETH

57 My part, I have resolved, O Lord,
   is to obey your word.
58 With all my heart I implore your favour;
   show the mercy of your promise.
59 I have pondered over my ways
   and returned to your will.
60 I made haste and did not delay
   to obey your commands.
61 Though the nets of the wicked ensnared me
   I remembered your law.
62 At midnight I will rise and thank you
   for your just decrees.
63 I am a friend of all who revere you,
   who obey your precepts.
64 Lord, your love fills the earth.
   Teach me your statutes.

TETH

65 Lord, you have been good to your servant
   according to your word.
66 Teach me discernment and knowledge
   for I trust in your commands.
67 Before I was afflicted I went astray
   but now I keep your word.
68 You are good and your deeds are good;
   teach me your statutes.
69 Though proud men smear me with lies
   yet I keep your precepts.
70 Their minds are closed to good
   but your law is my delight.
71 It was good for me to be afflicted,
   to learn your statutes.

72 The law from your mouth means more to me
than silver and gold.

YOD

73 It was your hands that made me and shaped me :
help me to learn your commands.
74 Your faithful will see me and rejoice
for I trust in your word.
75 Lord, I know that your decrees are right,
that you afflicted me justly.
76 Let your love be ready to console me
by your promise to your servant.
77 Let your love come to me and I shall live
for your law is my delight.
78 Shame the proud who harm me with lies
while I ponder your precepts.
79 Let your faithful turn to me,
those who know your will.
80 Let my heart be blameless in your statutes
lest I be ashamed.

CAPH

81 I yearn for your saving help;
I hope in your word.
82 My eyes yearn to see your promise.
When will you console me?
83 Though parched and exhausted with waiting
I remember your statutes.
84 How long must your servant suffer?
When will you sentence my oppressors?
85 For me the proud have dug pitfalls,
against your law.
86 Your commands are all true; then help me
when lies oppress me.
87 They almost made an end of me on earth
but I kept your precepts.
88 Because of your love give me life
and I will do your will.

LAMED

89 Your word, O Lord, for ever
stands firm in the heavens :

90 your truth lasts from age to age,
   like the earth you created.
91 By your decree it endures to this day;
   for all things serve you.
92 Had your law not been my delight
   I would have died in my affliction.
93 I will never forget your precepts
   for with them you give me life.
94 Save me, for I am yours
   since I seek your precepts.
95 Though the wicked lie in wait to destroy me
   yet I ponder on your will.
96 I have seen that all perfection has an end
   but your command is boundless.

MEM

97 Lord, how I love your law!
   It is ever in my mind.
98 Your command makes me wiser than my foes;
   for it is mine for ever.
99 I have more insight than all who teach me
   for I ponder your will.
100 I have more understanding than the old
    for I keep your precepts.
101 I turn my feet from evil paths
    to obey your word.
102 I have not turned away from your decrees;
    you yourself have taught me.
103 Your promise is sweeter to my taste
    than honey in the mouth.
104 I gain understanding from your precepts
    and so I hate false ways.

NUN

105 Your word is a lamp for my steps
    and a light for my path.
106 I have sworn and have determined
    to obey your decrees.
107 Lord, I am deeply afflicted:
    by your word give me life.
108 Accept, Lord, the homage of my lips
    and teach me your decrees.

109 Though I carry my life in my hands,
    I remember your law.

110 Though the wicked try to ensnare me
    I do not stray from your precepts.

111 Your will is my heritage for ever,
    the joy of my heart.

112 I set myself to carry out your statutes
    in fullness, for ever.

SAMECH

113 I have no love for half-hearted men:
    my love is for your law.

114 You are my shelter, my shield;
    I hope in your word.

115 Leave me, you who do evil;
    I will keep God's command.

116 If you uphold me by your promise I shall live;
    let my hopes not be in vain.

117 Sustain me and I shall be saved
    and ever observe your statutes.

118 You spurn all who swerve from your statutes;
    their cunning is in vain.

119 You throw away the wicked like dross:
    so I love your will.

120 I tremble before you in terror;
    I fear your decrees.

AYIN

121 I have done what is right and just:
    let me not be oppressed.

122 Vouch for the welfare of your servant
    lest the proud oppress me.

123 My eyes yearn for your saving help
    and the promise of your justice.

124 Treat your servant with love
    and teach me your statutes.

125 I am your servant, make me understand;
    then I shall know your will.

126 It is time for the Lord to act
    for your law has been broken.

127 That is why I love your commands
    more than finest gold.

128 That is why I rule my life by your precepts:
I hate false ways.

PE

129 Your will is wonderful indeed;
therefore I obey it.
130 The unfolding of your word gives light
and teaches the simple.
131 I open my mouth and I sigh
as I yearn for your commands.
132 Turn and show me your mercy;
show justice to your friends.
133 Let my steps be guided by your promise;
let no evil rule me.
134 Redeem me from man's oppression
and I will keep your precepts.
135 Let your face shine on your servant
and teach me your decrees.
136 Tears stream from my eyes
because your law is disobeyed.

SADE

137 Lord, you are just indeed;
your decrees are right.
138 You have imposed your will with justice
and with absolute truth.
139 I am carried away by anger
for my foes forget your word.
140 Your promise is tried in the fire,
the delight of your servant.
141 Although I am weak and despised
I remember your precepts.
142 Your justice is eternal justice
and your law is truth.
143 Though anguish and distress have seized me,
I delight in your commands.
144 The justice of your will is eternal:
if you teach me, I shall live.

KOPH

145 I call with all my heart; Lord, hear me,
I will keep your statutes.

146 I call upon you, save me
and I will do your will.
147 I rise before dawn and cry for help,
I hope in your word.
148 My eyes watch through the night
to ponder your promise.
149 In your love hear my voice, O Lord;
give me life by your decrees.
150 Those who harm me unjustly draw near:
they are far from your law.
151 But you, O Lord, are close:
your commands are truth.
152 Long have I known that your will
is established for ever.

RESH

153 See my affliction and save me
for I remember your law.
154 Uphold my cause and defend me;
by your promise, give me life.
155 Salvation is far from the wicked
who are heedless of your statutes.
156 Numberless, Lord, are your mercies;
with your decrees give me life.
157 Though my foes and oppressors are countless
I have not swerved from your will.
158 I look at the faithless with disgust;
they ignore your promise.
159 See how I love your precepts;
in your mercy give me life.
160 Your word is founded on truth:
your decrees are eternal.

SHIN

161 Though princes oppress me without cause
I stand in awe of your word.
162 I take delight in your promise
like one who finds a treasure.
163 Lies I hate and detest
but your law is my love.
164 Seven times a day I praise you
for your just decrees.

165 The lovers of your law have great peace;
   they never stumble.
166 I await your saving help, O Lord,
   I fulfil your commands.
167 My soul obeys your will
   and loves it dearly.
168 I obey your precepts and your will;
   all that I do is before you.

TAU

169 Lord, let my cry come before you:
   teach me by your word.
170 Let my pleading come before you;
   save me by your promise.
171 Let my lips proclaim your praise
   because you teach me your statutes.
172 Let my tongue sing your promise
   for your commands are just.
173 Let your hand be ready to help me,
   since I have chosen your precepts.
174 Lord, I long for your saving help
   and your law is my delight.
175 Give life to my soul that I may praise you.
   Let your decrees give me help.
176 I am lost like a sheep; seek your servant
   for I remember your commands.

119

Among treacherous strangers:
a pilgrimage song

1 To the Lord in the hour of my distress
  I call and he answers me.
2 "O Lord, save my soul from lying lips,
  from the tongue of the deceitful."

3 What shall he pay you in return,
  O treacherous tongue?
4 The warrior's arrows sharpened
  and coals, red-hot, blazing.

5 Alas, that I abide a stranger in Meshech,
  dwell among the tents of Kedar!

6 Long enough have I been dwelling
  with those who hate peace.
7 I am for peace, but when I speak,
  they are for fighting.

120

God the protector:
a pilgrimage song

1 I lift up my eyes to the mountains:
from where shall come my help?
2 My help shall come from the Lord
who made heaven and earth.

3 May he never allow you to stumble!
Let him sleep not, your guard.
4 No, he sleeps not nor slumbers,
Israel's guard.

5 The Lord is your guard and your shade;
at your right side he stands.
6 By day the sun shall not smite you
nor the moon in the night.

7 The Lord will guard you from evil,
he will guard your soul.
8 The Lord will guard your going and coming
both now and for ever.

121

Greeting to Jerusalem:
a pilgrimage song

1 I rejoiced when I heard them say:
  "Let us go to God's house."
2 And now our feet are standing
  within your gates, O Jerusalem.

3 Jerusalem is built as a city
  strongly compact.
4 It is there that the tribes go up,
  the tribes of the Lord.

  For Israel's law it is,
  there to praise the Lord's name.
5 There were set the thrones of judgment
  of the house of David.

6 For the peace of Jerusalem pray:
  "Peace be to your homes!
7 May peace reign in your walls,
  in your palaces, peace!"

8 For love of my brethren and friends
  I say: "Peace upon you!"
9 For love of the house of the Lord
  I will ask for your good.

122

Cry for help:
a pilgrimage song

1 To you have I lifted up my eyes,
 you who dwell in the heavens:
2 my eyes, like the eyes of slaves
 on the hand of their lords.

 Like the eyes of a servant
 on the hand of her mistress,
3 so our eyes are on the Lord our God
 till he show us his mercy.

4 Have mercy on us, Lord, have mercy.
 We are filled with contempt.
5 Indeed all too full is our soul
 with the scorn of the rich,
 (with the proud man's disdain).

123

Thanksgiving for help in crisis: a pilgrimage song

1 " If the Lord had not been on our side,"
 this is Israel's song.
2 " If the Lord had not been on our side
 when men rose against us,
3 then would they have swallowed us alive
 when their anger was kindled.

4 Then would the waters have engulfed us,
 the torrent gone over us;
5 over our head would have swept
 the raging waters."

6 Blessed be the Lord who did not give us
 a prey to their teeth!
7 Our life, like a bird, has escaped
 from the snare of the fowler.

 Indeed the snare has been broken
 and we have escaped.
8 Our help is in the name of the Lord,
 who made heaven and earth.

124

Unshakable faith:
a pilgrimage song

1 Those who put their trust in the Lord
  are like Mount Sion, that cannot be shaken,
  that stands for ever.

2 Jerusalem! The mountains surround her,
  so the Lord surrounds his people
  both now and for ever.

3 For the sceptre of the wicked shall not rest
  over the land of the just
  for fear that the hands of the just
  should turn to evil.

4 Do good, Lord, to those who are good,
  to the upright of heart;
5 but the crooked and those who do evil,
  drive them away!

  On Israel, peace!

125

Song of the returned exiles:
a pilgrimage song

1 When the Lord delivered Sion from bondage,
   It seemed like a dream.
2 Then was our mouth filled with laughter,
   on our lips there were songs.

   The heathens themselves said: "What marvels
   the Lord worked for them!"
3 What marvels the Lord worked for us!
   Indeed we were glad.

4 Deliver us, O Lord, from our bondage
   as streams in dry land.
5 Those who are sowing in tears
   will sing when they reap.

6 They go out, they go out, full of tears,
   carrying seed for the sowing:
   they come back, they come back, full of song,
   carrying their sheaves.

126

Success depends on God's blessing:
a pilgrimage song

1 If the Lord does not build the house,
in vain do its builders labour;
if the Lord does not watch over the city,
in vain does the watchman keep vigil.

2 In vain is your earlier rising,
your going later to rest,
you who toil for the bread you eat:
when he pours gifts on his beloved while they slumber.

3 Truly sons are a gift from the Lord,
a blessing, the fruit of the womb.
4 Indeed the sons of youth
are like arrows in the hand of a warrior.

5 O the happiness of the man
who has filled his quiver with these arrows!
He will have no cause for shame
when he disputes with his foes in the gateways.

127

The blessings of home:
a pilgrimage song

1 O blessed are those who fear the Lord
   and walk in his ways!

2 By the labour of your hands you shall eat.
   You will be happy and prosper;
3 your wife like a fruitful vine
   in the heart of your house;
   your children like shoots of the olive,
   around your table.

4 Indeed thus shall be blessed
   the man who fears the Lord.
5 May the Lord bless you from Sion
5c all the days of your life!
6 May you see your children's children
5b in a happy Jerusalem!

   On Israel, peace!

128

The fate of Israel's enemies:
a pilgrimage song

1 "They have pressed me hard from my youth,"
this is Israel's song.
2 "They have pressed me hard from my youth
but could never destroy me.

3 They ploughed my back like ploughmen,
drawing long furrows.
4 But the Lord who is just, has destroyed
the yoke of the wicked."

5 Let them be shamed and routed,
those who hate Sion!
6 Let them be like grass on the roof
that withers before it flowers.

7 With that no reaper fills his arms,
no binder makes his sheaves
8 and those passing by will not say:
"On you the Lord's blessing!"

"We bless you in the name of the Lord."

129

Prayer of repentance and trust:
sixth psalm of repentance

1 Out of the depths I cry to you, O Lord,
2 Lord, hear my voice!
  O let your ears be attentive
  to the voice of my pleading.

3 If you, O Lord, should mark our guilt,
  Lord, who would survive?
4 But with you is found forgiveness:
  for this we revere you.

5 My soul is waiting for the Lord,
  I count on his word.
6 My soul is longing for the Lord
  more than watchman for daybreak.
  (Let the watchman count on daybreak
7 and Israel on the Lord.)

  Because with the Lord there is mercy
  and fullness of redemption,
8 Israel indeed he will redeem
  from all its iniquity.

130

Song of serenity:
a pilgrimage song

1 O Lord, my heart is not proud
nor haughty my eyes.
I have not gone after things too great
nor marvels beyond me.

2 Truly I have set my soul
in silence and peace.
A weaned child on its mother's breast,
even so is my soul.

3 O Israel, hope in the Lord
both now and for ever.

131

God's promise to David:
a pilgrimage song

1 O Lord, remember David
   and all the hardships he endured,
2 the oath he swore to the Lord,
   his vow to the Strong One of Jacob.

3 "I will not enter the house where I live
   nor go to the bed where I rest.
4 I will give no sleep to my eyes
   to my eyelids will give no slumber
5 till I find a place for the Lord,
   a dwelling for the Strong One of Jacob."

6 At Ephrata we heard of the ark;
   we found it in the plains of Yearim.
7 "Let us go to the place of his dwelling;
   let us go to kneel at his footstool."

8 Go up, Lord, to the place of your rest,
   you and the ark of your strength.
9 Your priests shall be clothed with holiness:
   your faithful shall ring out their joy.
10 For the sake of David your servant
   do not reject your anointed.

11 The Lord swore an oath to David;
   he will not go back on his word:
   "A son, the fruit of your body,
   will I set upon your throne.

12 If they keep my covenant in truth
   and my laws that I have taught them,
   their sons also shall rule
   on your throne from age to age."

13 For the Lord has chosen Sion;
   he has desired it for his dwelling:
14 "This is my resting-place for ever,
   here have I chosen to live.

15 I will greatly bless her produce,
   I will fill her poor with bread.
16 I will clothe her priests with salvation
   and her faithful shall ring out their joy.

17 There the stock of David will flower:
   I will prepare a lamp for my anointed.
18 I will cover his enemies with shame
   but on him my crown shall shine."

132

The blessings of unity:
a pilgrimage song

1 How good and how pleasant it is,
   brothers dwelling in unity!

2 It is like precious oil upon the head
   running down upon the beard,
   running down upon Aaron's beard
   upon the collar of his robes.

3 It is like the dew of Hermon which falls
   on the heights of Sion.
   For there the Lord gives his blessing,
   life for ever.

133

Prayer at night-time:
a pilgrimage song

1 O come, bless the Lord,
   all you who serve the Lord,
   who stand in the house of the Lord,
   in the courts of the house of our God.
2 Lift up your hands to the holy place
   and bless the Lord through the night.

3 May the Lord bless you from Sion,
   he who made both heaven and earth.

134

Anthology of praise

1 Alleluia!

Praise the name of the Lord,
praise him, servants of the Lord,
2 who stand in the house of the Lord
in the courts of the house of our God.

3 Praise the Lord for the Lord is good.
Sing a psalm to his name for he is loving.
4 For the Lord has chosen Jacob for himself
and Israel for his own possession.

5 For I know the Lord is great,
that our Lord is high above all gods.
6 The Lord does whatever he wills,
in heaven, on earth, in the seas.

7 He summons clouds from the ends of the earth;
makes lightning produce the rain;
from his treasuries he sends forth the wind.

8 The first-born of the Egyptians he smote,
of man and beast alike.
9 Signs and wonders he worked
in the midst of your land, O Egypt,
against Pharaoh and all his servants.

10 Nations in their greatness he struck
and kings in their splendour he slew.
11 Sihon, king of the Amorites,
Og, the king of Bashan,
and all the kingdoms of Canaan.
12 He let Israel inherit their land;
on his people their land he bestowed.

13 Lord, your name stands for ever,
unforgotten from age to age:
14 for the Lord does justice for his people;
the Lord takes pity on his servants.

15 Pagan idols are silver and gold,
the work of human hands.
16 They have mouths but they cannot speak;
they have eyes but they cannot see.

17 They have ears but they cannot hear;
there is never a breath on their lips.
18 Their makers will become like them
and so will all who trust in them!

19 Sons of Israel, bless the Lord!
Sons of Aaron, bless the Lord!
20 Sons of Levi, bless the Lord!
You who fear him, bless the Lord!

21 From Sion may the Lord be blessed,
he who dwells in Jerusalem!

135

Litany of praises:
psalm of worship

1 Alleluia!
   O give thanks to the Lord for he is good,
   for his great love is without end.
2 Give thanks to the God of gods,
   for his great love is without end.
3 Give thanks to the Lord of lords,
   for his great love is without end;

4 who alone has wrought marvellous works,
   for his great love is without end;
5 whose wisdom it was made the skies,
   for his great love is without end;
6 who fixed the earth firmly on the seas,
   for his great love is without end.

7 It was he who made the great lights,
   for his great love is without end,
8 the sun to rule in the day,
   for his great love is without end,
9 the moon and stars in the night,
   for his great love is without end.

10 The first-born of the Egyptians he smote,
   for his great love is without end.
11 He brought Israel out from their midst,
   for his great love is without end;
12 arm outstretched, with power in his hand,
   for his great love is without end.

13 He divided the Red Sea in two,
   for his great love is without end;
14 he made Israel pass through the midst,
   for his great love is without end;
15 he flung Pharaoh and his force in the sea,
   for his great love is without end.

16 Through the desert his people he led,
  for his great love is without end.
17 Nations in their greatness he struck,
  for his great love is without end.
18 Kings in their splendour he slew,
  for his great love is without end.

19 Sihon, king of the Amorites,
  for his great love is without end
20 and Og, the king of Bashan,
  for his great love is without end.

21 He let Israel inherit their land,
  for his great love is without end.
22 On his servant their land he bestowed,
  for his great love is without end.
23 He remembered us in our distress,
  for his great love is without end.

24 And he snatched us away from our foes,
  for his great love is without end.
25 He gives food to all living things,
  for his great love is without end.
26 To the God of heaven give thanks,
  for his great love is without end.

136

Homesickness in exile

1 By the rivers of Babylon
  there we sat and wept,
  remembering Sion;
2 on the poplars that grew there
  we hung up our harps.

3 For it was there that they asked us,
  our captors, for songs,
  our oppressors, for joy.
  "Sing to us," they said,
  "one of Sion's songs."

4 O how could we sing
  the song of the Lord
  on alien soil?
5 If I forget you, Jerusalem,
  let my right hand wither!

6 O let my tongue
  cleave to my mouth
  if I remember you not,
  if I prize not Jerusalem
  above all my joys!

7 Remember, O Lord,
  against the sons of Edom
  the day of Jerusalem;
  when they said : "Tear it down!
  Tear it down to its foundations!"

8 O Babylon, destroyer,
  he is happy who repays you
  the ills you brought on us.
9 He shall seize and shall dash
  your children on the rock!

137

Thanksgiving to a faithful God

1 I thank you, Lord, with all my heart,
you have heard the words of my mouth.
Before the angels I will bless you.
2 I will adore before your holy temple.

 I thank you for your faithfulness and love
which excel all we ever knew of you.
3 On the day I called, you answered;
you increased the strength of my soul.

4 All earth's kings shall thank you
when they hear the words of your mouth.
5 They shall sing of the Lord's ways:
"How great is the glory of the Lord!"

6 The Lord is high yet he looks on the lowly
and the haughty he knows from afar.
7 Though I walk in the midst of affliction
you give me life and frustrate my foes.

 You stretch out your hand and save me,
your hand 8 will do all things for me.
Your love, O Lord, is eternal,
discard not the work of your hands.

138

The Hound of Heaven

1 O Lord, you search me and you know me,
2 you know my resting and my rising,
    you discern my purpose from afar.
3 You mark when I walk or lie down,
    all my ways lie open to you.

4 Before ever a word is on my tongue
    you know it, O Lord, through and through.
5 Behind and before you besiege me,
    your hand ever laid upon me.
6 Too wonderful for me, this knowledge,
    too high, beyond my reach.

7 O where can I go from your spirit,
    or where can I flee from your face?
8 If I climb the heavens, you are there.
    If I lie in the grave, you are there.

9 If I take the wings of the dawn
    and dwell at the sea's furthest end,
10 even there your hand would lead me,
    your right hand would hold me fast.

11 If I say: "Let the darkness hide me
    and the light around me be night,"
12 even darkness is not dark for you
    and the night is as clear as the day.

13 For it was you who created my being,
    knit me together in my mother's womb.
14 I thank you for the wonder of my being,
    for the wonders of all your creation.

    Already you knew my soul,
15 my body held no secret from you
    when I was being fashioned in secret
    and moulded in the depths of the earth.

16 Your eyes saw all my actions,
  they were all of them written in your book;
  every one of my days was decreed
  before one of them came into being.

17 To me, how mysterious your thoughts,
  the sum of them not to be numbered!
18 If I count them, they are more than the sand;
  to finish, I must be eternal, like you.

19 O God, that you would slay the wicked!
  Men of blood, keep far away from me!
20 with deceit they rebel against you
  and set your designs at naught.

21 Do I not hate those who hate you,
  abhor those who rise against you?
22 I hate them with a perfect hate
  and they are foes to me.

23 O search me, God, and know my heart.
  O test me and know my thoughts.
24 See that I follow not the wrong path
  and lead me in the path of life eternal.

139

Prayer under persecution

2 Rescue me, Lord, from evil men;
   from the violent keep me safe,
3 from those who plan evil in their hearts
   and stir up strife every day;
4 who sharpen their tongue like an adder's,
   with the poison of viper on their lips.

5 Lord, guard me from the hands of the wicked;
   from the violent keep me safe;
   they plan to make me stumble.
6 The proud have hidden a trap,
   have spread out lines in a net,
   set snares across my path.

7 I have said to the Lord: "You are my God."
   Lord, hear the cry of my appeal!
8 Lord my God, my mighty help,
   you shield my head in the battle.
9 Do not grant the wicked their desire
   nor let their plots succeed.

10 Those surrounding me lift up their heads.
   Let the malice of their speech overwhelm them.
11 Let coals of fire rain upon them.
   Let them be flung in the abyss, no more to rise.
12 Let the slanderer not endure upon the earth.
   Let evil hunt the violent man to death!

13 I know that the Lord will avenge the poor,
   that he will do justice for the needy.
   Truly the just will praise your name:
   the upright shall live in your presence.

140

Evening prayer for protection

1 I have called to you, Lord; hasten to help me!
  Hear my voice when I cry to you.
2 Let my prayer come before you like incense,
  the raising of my hands like an evening oblation.

3 Lord, set a guard over my mouth;
  keep watch at the door of my lips!
4 Do not turn my heart to things that are wrong,
  to evil deeds with men who are sinners.

  Never allow me to share in their feasting.
5 If a good man strikes or reproves me it is kindness;
  but let the oil of the wicked not anoint my head.
  Let my prayer be ever against their malice.

6 Their princes were thrown down by the side of the
    rock:
  then they understood that my words were kind.
7 As a millstone is shattered to pieces on the ground,
  so their bones were strewn at the mouth of the grave.

8 To you, Lord God, my eyes are turned:
  in you I take refuge; spare my soul!
9 From the trap they have laid for me keep me safe:
  keep me from the snares of those who do evil.

10 Let the wicked fall into the traps they have set
  whilst I pursue my way unharmed.

141

Prayer of a man deserted by his friends

2 With all my voice I cry to the Lord,
  with all my voice I entreat the Lord.
3 I pour out my trouble before him;
  I tell him all my distress
4 while my spirit faints within me.
  But you, O Lord, know my path.

  On the way where I shall walk
  they have hidden a snare to entrap me.
5 Look on my right and see:
  there is not one who takes my part.
  I have no means of escape,
  not one who cares for my soul.

6 I cry to you, O Lord.
  I have said: "You are my refuge,
  all I have left in the land of the living."
7 Listen then to my cry
  for I am in the depths of distress.

  Rescue me from those who pursue me
  for they are stronger than I.
8 Bring my soul out of this prison
  and then I shall praise your name.
  Around me the just will assemble
  because of your goodness to me.

142

Prayer in desolation:
seventh psalm of repentance

1 Lord, listen to my prayer:
  turn your ear to my appeal.
  You are faithful, you are just; give answer.
2 Do not call your servant to judgment
  for no one is just in your sight.

3 The enemy pursues my soul;
  he has crushed my life to the ground;
  he has made me dwell in darkness
  like the dead, long forgotten.
4 Therefore my spirit fails;
  my heart is numb within me.

5 I remember the days that are past:
  I ponder all your works.
  I muse on what your hand has wrought
6 and to you I stretch out my hands.
  Like a parched land my soul thirsts for you.

7 Lord, make haste and give me answer;
  for my spirit fails within me.
  Do not hide your face
  lest I become like those in the grave.

8 In the morning let me know your love
  for I put my trust in you.
  Make me know the way I should walk:
  to you I lift up my soul.

9 Rescue me, Lord, from my enemies;
  I have fled to you for refuge.
10 Teach me to do your will
  for you, O Lord, are my God.
  Let your good spirit guide me
  in ways that are level and smooth.

11 For your name's sake, Lord, save my life;
   in your justice save my soul from distress.
12 In your love make an end of my foes;
   destroy all those who oppress me
   for I am your servant, O Lord.

143

Appeal for victory and peace

1 Blessed be the Lord, my rock
who trains my arms for battle,
who prepares my hands for war.

2 He is my love, my fortress;
he is my stronghold, my saviour,
my shield, my place of refuge.
He brings peoples under my rule.

3 Lord, what is man that you care for him,
mortal man, that you keep him in mind;
4 man, who is merely a breath
whose life fades like a passing shadow?

5 Lower your heavens and come down;
touch the mountains; wreathe them in smoke.
6 Flash your lightnings; rout the foe,
shoot your arrows and put them to flight.

7 Reach down from heaven and save me;
draw me out from the mighty waters,
from the hands of alien foes
8 whose mouths are filled with lies,
whose hands are raised in perjury.

9 To you, O God, will I sing a new song;
I will play on the ten-stringed lute
10 to you who give kings their victory,
who set David your servant free.

11 You set him free from the evil sword;
you rescued him from alien foes
whose mouths were filled with lies,
whose hands were raised in perjury.

*　　*　　*

12 Let our sons then flourish like saplings
grown tall and strong from their youth:
our daughters graceful as columns,
adorned as though for a palace.

13 Let our barns be filled to overflowing
with crops of every kind;
our sheep increasing by thousands,
myriads of sheep in our fields,
14 our cattle heavy with young,

no ruined wall, no exile,
no sound of weeping in our streets.
15 Happy the people with such blessings;
happy the people whose God is the Lord.

144

Praise of God's grandeur:
an alphabetical psalm

1 I will give you glory, O God my King,
  I will bless your name for ever.

2 I will bless you day after day
  and praise your name for ever.
3 The Lord is great, highly to be praised,
  his greatness cannot be measured.

4 Age to age shall proclaim your works,
  shall declare your mighty deeds,
5 shall speak of your splendour and glory,
  tell the tale of your wonderful works.

6 They will speak of your terrible deeds,
  recount your greatness and might.
7 They will recall your abundant goodness;
  age to age shall ring out your justice.

8 The Lord is kind and full of compassion,
  slow to anger, abounding in love.
9 How good is the Lord to all,
  compassionate to all his creatures.

10 All your creatures shall thank you, O Lord,
   and your friends shall repeat their blessing.
11 They shall speak of the glory of your reign
   and declare your might, O God,

12 to make known to men your mighty deeds
   and the glorious splendour of your reign.
13 Yours is an everlasting kingdom;
   your rule lasts from age to age.

   The Lord is faithful in all his words
   and loving in all his deeds.
14 The Lord supports all who fall
   and raises all who are bowed down.

15 The eyes of all creatures look to you
   and you give them their food in due time.
16 You open wide your hand,
   grant the desires of all who live.

17 The Lord is just in all his ways
   and loving in all his deeds.
18 He is close to all who call him,
   who call on him from their hearts.

19 He grants the desires of those who fear him,
   he hears their cry and he saves them.
20 The Lord protects all who love him;
   but the wicked he will utterly destroy.

21 Let me speak the praise of the Lord,
   let all mankind bless his holy name
   for ever, for ages unending.

145

Praise of God's fidelity

1 Alleluia!

My soul, give praise to the Lord;
2 I will praise the Lord all my days,
make music to my God while I live.

3 Put no trust in princes,
in mortal men in whom there is no help.
4 Take their breath, they return to clay
and their plans that day come to nothing.

5 He is happy who is helped by Jacob's God,
whose hope is in the Lord his God,
6 who alone made heaven and earth,
the seas and all they contain.

It is he who keeps faith for ever,
7 who is just to those who are oppressed.
It is he who gives bread to the hungry,
the Lord, who sets prisoners free,

8 the Lord who gives sight to the blind,
who raises up those who are bowed down,
9 the Lord, who protects the stranger
and upholds the widow and orphan.

8c It is the Lord who loves the just
9c but thwarts the path of the wicked.
10 The Lord will reign for ever,
Sion's God, from age to age.

Alleluia!

146

Praise to God who maintains the world

1 Alleluia!

Praise the Lord for he is good;
sing to our God for he is loving:
to him our praise is due.

2 The Lord builds up Jerusalem
and brings back Israel's exiles,
3 he heals the broken-hearted,
he binds up all their wounds.
4 He fixes the number of the stars;
he calls each one by its name.

5 Our Lord is great and almighty;
his wisdom can never be measured.
6 The Lord raises the lowly;
he humbles the wicked to the dust.
7 Sing to the Lord, giving thanks;
sing psalms to our God with the harp.

8 He covers the heavens with clouds;
he prepares the rain for the earth,
making mountains sprout with grass
and with plants to serve man's needs.
9 He provides the beasts with their food
and young ravens that call upon him.

10 His delight is not in horses
nor his pleasure in warriors' strength.
11 The Lord delights in those who revere him,
in those who wait for his love.

147

Praise of God's personal care for Israel

12 O praise the Lord, Jerusalem!
Sion, praise your God!

13 He has strengthened the bars of your gates,
he has blessed the children within you
14 He established peace on your borders,
he feeds you with finest wheat.

15 He sends out his word to the earth
and swiftly runs his command.
16 He showers down snow white as wool
he scatters hoar-frost like ashes.

17 He hurls down hailstones like crumbs.
The waters are frozen at his touch;
18 he sends forth his word and it melts them:
at the breath of his mouth the waters flow.

19 He makes his word known to Jacob,
to Israel his laws and decrees.
20 He has not dealt thus with other nations;
he has not taught them his decrees.

Alleluia!

148

Cosmic praise

1 Alleluia!

Praise the Lord from the heavens,
praise him in the heights.
2 Praise him, all his angels,
praise him, all his host.

3 Praise him, sun and moon,
praise him, shining stars.
4 Praise him, highest heavens
and the waters above the heavens.

5 Let them praise the name of the Lord.
He commanded: they were made.
6 He fixed them for ever,
gave a law which shall not pass away.

7 Praise the Lord from the earth,
sea creatures and all oceans,
8 fire and hail, snow and mist,
stormy winds that obey his word;

9 all mountains and hills,
all fruit trees and cedars,
10 beasts, wild and tame,
reptiles and birds on the wing;

11 all earth's kings and peoples,
earth's princes and rulers;
12 young men and maidens,
old men together with children.

13 Let them praise the name of the Lord
for he alone is exalted.
The splendour of his name
reaches beyond heaven and earth.

14 He exalts the strength of his people.
He is the praise of all his saints,
of the sons of Israel,
of the people to whom he comes close.

Alleluia!

149

Praise to the God of victories

1 Alleluia!

  Sing a new song to the Lord,
  his praise in the assembly of the faithful.
2 Let Israel rejoice in its Maker,
  let Sion's sons exult in their king.
3 Let them praise his name with dancing
  and make music with timbrel and harp.

4 For the Lord takes delight in his people.
  He crowns the poor with salvation.
5 Let the faithful rejoice in their glory,
  shout for joy and take their rest.
6 Let the praise of God be on their lips
  and a two-edged sword in their hand,

7 to deal out vengeance to the nations
  and punishment on all the peoples;
8 to bind their kings in chains
  and their nobles in fetters of iron;
9 to carry out the sentence pre-ordained:
  this honour is for all his faithful.

  Alleluia!

150

Final summons to praise

1 Alleluia!

Praise God in his holy place,
praise him in his mighty heavens.
2 Praise him for his powerful deeds,
praise his surpassing greatness.

3 O praise him with sound of trumpet,
praise him with lute and harp.
4 Praise him with timbrel and dance,
praise him with strings and pipes.

5 O praise him with resounding cymbals,
praise him with clashing of cymbals.
6 Let everything that lives and that breathes
give praise to the Lord. Alleluia!

The numbering of the psalms to be found in most Christian liturgies is taken from the Greek Septuagint. This numeration differs from that found in the Hebrew text and the Authorised Version. Since books with a liturgical emphasis (such as the present one) generally follow the Septuagint numbering, and other Biblical and exegetical works the Hebrew, it seems useful to give the comparative numbering of the two systems:

Greek Septuagint	Hebrew
1–8	1–8
9	9–10
10–112	11–113
113	114–115
114–115	116
116–145	117–146
146–147	147
148–150	148–150

Therefore for most of the psalms the Greek numeration is one behind that of the Hebrew.

The numbering of the verses is also slightly different from that of the later English versions. These generally begin numbering the verses from the body of the psalm, and leave its preceding title out of account. The liturgical texts on the other hand have included the title in their reckoning, and when this is more than a few words long, they have counted the beginning of the psalm as its second or third verse. It is this latter system which has been followed here, though the wording of the titles themselves has not been included. Very occasionally the sequence of verses within a psalm has been disturbed (as for instance in psalm 21:16-18) in an attempt to restore what appears to have been the order of the original.

Musical editions of many of
these psalms, and gramo-
phone records, may be ob-
tained from *The Grail*, 58
Sloane Street, London, s.w.1